SORRY I'M STREAMING
WHY YOU SHOULD
CREATE YOUR OWN
NETFLIX
AND HOW TO PULL IT OFF

YOUR STEP BY STEP GUIDE TO GETTING YOUR PIECE OF THE VIDEO STREAMING WEALTH POOL

BY AMAZON #1 BEST SELLING AUTHOR
ANTONIO T SMITH JR

Sorry, I'm Streaming

Why You Should Create Your Own Netflix and How To Pull It Off

Your Step By Step Guide To Getting Your Piece Of The Video Streaming Wealth Pool

Connect With Me

Join our online community to stay inspired, network, and to find our ATS Community. Visit

VYBN: https://sharingourwealth.com/social/theatsjr

Text Me At +1-409-500-1546

The Cozy Corner Speakers Group can bring authors to your live events. For more information or to book an event, contact us at

speakersgroup@cozycornerpublishing.com

Cozy Corner
Publishing

Cozy Corner Publishing
A publication of Cozy Corner Publishing
Galveston, TX
©2021 by Cozy Corner Publishing

Sorry, I'm Streaming:
Why You Should Create Your Own Netflix and How To Pull It Off
Your Step By Step Guide To Getting Your Piece Of The Video Streaming Wealth Pool

Sorry, I'm Streaming   Antonio T. Smith, Jr.

Contents

&

Introduction

Imagine finding an oil well at the height of the fossil fuel industry's boom. Imagine finding a gold reserve in your backyard during the gold rush. Imagine having the largest social network right around the big tech boom. It really is something to be in the right place at the right time when an industry is experiencing a boom. But it is often visible only in hindsight.

In fact, sometimes people are betting against what is undeniably the future of a market. Can you believe that Kodak, the leader of analog photography, came up with the first digital camera? Yes, the corporation got taken out by the thing they invented. They just did not know that it was the thing to put their weight behind. They doubled down on analog, and before they knew it, companies like Sony were taking massive chunks of their market share, and they had already invested tens of millions into analog technology destined to fail.

In hindsight, there are always signs that could've been seen as the dawn of a new industry, yet there are only a few who cash in. "If only someone told me to invest in bitcoin," many say when they encounter someone who has built a fortune buying bitcoins for less than a dollar. What if I were to tell you that we are in the age of yet another industry, and you have the opportunity to cash in?

In May of 2020, the world learned that independent content creator Joe Rogan had signed an exclusive licensing deal for his content with Spotify. The value of the deal? A hundred million dollars. And that spelled the beginning of the content industry's rise. As soon as Rogan signed on the dotted line, we entered a new world. The beginnings of this world go all the way back to Disney's then CEO Bob Iger acquiring Pixar from Steve Jobs back in 2006. Value of the deal? $7.4 billion.

While corporations and media conglomerates were in the content game forever, it is around the age of streaming introduced by Netflix that these giants started cutting in smaller content creators. And as soon people learned about the Rogan deal, they should have hopped on the content creation wagon right away. As late as it may seem, the time is now.

For anyone with personality, charm, and charisma, it is time to start an interview show. For anyone with a flair for the dramatic, it is time to get involved in the fiction media space. And for anyone with money to invest, it is time to build your own Netflix. In this book, I will cover content creation as well as platform building. And I will make a solid case for why you could realistically be the next streaming millionaire and possibly a billionaire if you use the right tools and strategies. Like music? Get started on that. Like sports? Get started on that. Like self-development? Get started on that. It does not matter what your interests are; you have the opportunity to get your share of the subscription video on demand pie.

STEP ONE

INVESTIGATE

OWNERSHIP

)*

Who Owns the News?

Quite some time has passed since people seriously considered who owns a controlling interest in the businesses that deliver the news. Since truth gets measured by what news media reports and news media are for-profit businesses, there is a fundamental conflict of interest.

However, as capitalism does with anything, we leave it for the competition to iron out the problems. In other words, if a channel lies to the public, the viewers will switch to another channel that is more honest and accurate in its reporting.

Guess what? 13 people own a majority of the country's news media. Don't believe me? I am not pushing a conspiracy theory, these are their names, and they have publicly listed ownership and or control of pretty much all the news you consume.

1. Michael Bloomberg owns Bloomberg LP and Bloomberg Media.

2. Rupert Murdoch owns News Corp (and 120 Newspapers alongside his family). Some notable names that are or have been under his influence include The New York Times, The Wall Street Journal, Fox News, and 21 Century Fox.

3. Donald and Si Newhouse control Advance Publications. Some names that may be familiar to you include Wired magazine, The New Yorker, Vogue, and Vanity Fair.

))

4. The Cox Family controls the Atlanta Journal-Constitution (giving them the ownership and control of 14 TV channels and 59 radio stations).

5. Jeff Bezos bought The Washington Post in 2013.

6. John Henry controls The Boston Globe.

7. Sheldon Adelson controls The Las Vegas Review-Journal.

8. Joe Mansueto controls Inc. and Fast Company magazines.

9. Mortimer Zuckerman controls US News, World Report, and New York Daily News.

10. Barbey Family controls Village Voice.

11. Stanley Hubbard controls Hubbard Broadcasting, which gives him control of 13 TV channels, including local affiliates of ABC and NBC News.

12. Carlon Slim Helu controls The New York Times with the largest individual stake.

13. Warren Buffet has invested in regional daily papers, a company that has over 70 dailies as of today.

As you can see, some companies own dozens of news outlets and television stations, giving you the illusion of variety and competition. But if fifteen or so people decide that a certain story is true, it is nearly impossible for the American public to believe otherwise.

My point of bringing this up is not to spell doom and gloom but to highlight the opportunity. Remember that in capitalism,

)!

market corrections are the rule, not the exception. If companies get overvalued, the value crashes to correct for the hype. If companies are undervalued, a correction happens, and the value increases. One thing that often gets corrected is that when too much power gets in the hand of too few people. Democratization occurs spontaneously, and those who anticipate it are at the forefront of cashing in on the opportunity. Uber did it with the cab industry, AirBnB did it with the hoteling industry, and you can do it with the news industry. If you start as little as a blog, you are taking a first step towards becoming a part of this revolution. And you have no idea what someone might pay you to buy it off.

)"

Who Owns the Entertainment?

While with news channels, the ownership of media companies seems to be from behind smokes and mirrors, with entertainment conglomerates love to throw their names at you right at the beginning of movies. You may still not fully grasp how much of your media is owned by a small number of companies. So in this chapter, I will cover the six or so companies that have an oligopoly on your entertainment.

A conversation about this cannot possibly be started without discussing Disney. Before recently stepping down from Disney, the former CEO Bob Iger led a mission of acquiring high-value entertainment properties that covered pretty much every name you are familiar with. As of today, Disney owns ABC, 80% of ESPN, Touchstone Pictures, Marvel, Lucas Film (everything Star Wars), 50% of A&E, 50% of The History Channel, 50% of Lifetime, Pixar, Hollywood Records, 10% of Vice Media, Core Publishing, and 21st Century Fox.

So everything from rightwing talk shows like the one on Fox News to leftist late-night TV shows, like Jimmy Kimmel Live, are owned by Disney. And here's what makes their ownership interesting: they don't just own these companies, they own the content, and that's what is valuable. That is why when Disney launched its streaming service Disney Plus, the plus stood for content from all the companies Disney had bought in its acquisition strategy. As of today, the platform owned by a single company has over five hundred films and seven thousand episodes of television.

Moving away from Disney, we have Viacom. The restructured company is now called ViacomCBS, and here are some of its properties: CBS, All the Showtime Channels, Paramount Pictures, Nickelodeon MTV, Comedy Central, BET, CBS All Access, Pluto TV, and the publishing house Simon & Schuster. Instead of listing out the number of movies and shows owned by the company, it suffices to say that the giant owns 170 networks that reach 700 million people.

If you have had enough of Disney and ViacomCBS, you can feast on the content galore owned by Marner Media. Formerly Time Warner, this media conglomerate itself is owned by AT&T, which was founded by Alexander Graham Bell, the inventor of the telephone. A company as old as AT&T knows a thing or two about investing and its media entity TimeWarner owns Warner Bros., The CW, Fandango Media (which includes Rotten Tomatoes, Turner Entertainment, WaterTower Music, New Line Cinema, DC Films, TMZ, HBO, Cartoon Network, and CNN among other media companies.

This conglomerate doesn't just own movie studios; it also owns a network of sites that review movies. I hope that by diving into the kind of ownership a handful of companies have over our entertainment, I have illustrated that we are due for a correction. And even if we are not, it must be motivating for you to know that the people buying content rights have deep pockets and billions of dollars to spare. So I encourage you that instead of breaking your back to build a brick and mortar company that you will sell to a small fry millionaire, start laying the foundation for your streaming business that you can sell to multi-billion dollar giants.

It Always Ends With People

The temptation to see corporations as alien is there when we discuss control and ownership. After all, no one wants to believe that a few humans have so much power. But it is important that you understand that it is not just three conglomerates who own most of your entertainment and news; it is less than fifty humans. Thirty-two media executives control the information consumed by over 277 million Americans. That means one executive decides what 850,000 people view.

Of course, this is done through a complex media machinery housed under a number of companies, but you have to realize that it is the same six companies that own 70% of the cable you watch. We discussed TimeWarner in the previous chapter, and 200 million unique users read news published by its properties. We believe readership is going away while media conglomerates won't even spare radio. There is a company called Clear Channel, and it owns not five hundred, not one thousand but a whopping twelve hundred radio stations. One company. And guess who runs that one company? People.

They are people, and you are a person. How much news do you control? The answer is most likely zero. But if you curate what you share on Facebook, you control 0.00000000001% of your friends' news diet. How much entertainment do you own? The answer is likely zero, but if you have a podcast, you own a tiny portion of the overall streaming pie.

This first part has been about convincing you that this industry is booming and that there are buyers everywhere. If you start something that gets hot enough, it will be taken off your hands, and you will be paid handsomely. And if you want to create your own economy by not just owning content but expanding it into a full-fledged streaming platform, then more power to you; I will teach you how to do that as well.

But it has to start with the people. Remember who you are as a person and pick something for content creation that resonates with you. It is easy to dismiss media executives as cold calculating empty suits, but you have to realize how much passion Bob Iger had for different kinds of stories and Disney mythology as a whole to rise from heading a company under Disney to rising to the conglomerate's CEO. And afterward, the man talked some of the most artistic independents into selling their companies to him. Who else got Steve Jobs and George Lucas on board.

If Billion Dollar Bob has to be a human at the top of the media game, you cannot afford to make empty content with dollar signs in your eyes. You have to start with genuine content that will come from you, the person, and resonate with your audience, the people. And eventually, you will either sell it to billion-dollar corporations run by people or take it public on a stock market led by people. Just remember that it all ends with people, and people love authenticity. Remember who you are, and that will be your unique selling point forever.

STEP TWO

LEARN ABOUT

THE MARKET

Stop Making History

In our lives, we have heard people insist that making history is a great thing. But Kodak was busy investing in technology that was history; that is why Kodak became history. Nokia was busy sticking with the Symbian operating system, which belonged in history. The result was Nokia becoming history. Television today is facing a similar fate. While it has a foot in the present, it quite clearly belongs in the past, and those who continue to make it or invest in it are firmly placing themselves to be left behind.

Usually, there is a clear sign, writing on the wall that declares when there's a change in the guard. If all major TV studios throwing their weight behind streaming platforms wasn't a declaration of the old guard's time being up, let the story of Quibi hammer home the point.

Quibi was meant to be a streaming app that catered to young people with shows of up to ten minutes in length. Yes, the streaming platform was meant to attract those with an attention span as short as ten minutes. And people were supposed to pay for this service. Guess how much it raised in funding? Nearly two billion dollars. That is the kind of faith venture capitalists and money people have in the future of streaming.

The app failed because of several reasons, and one of them was that they invested heavily in A-list TV celebrities. Guess what? No one cares about TV celebrities anymore. That's spending money on history. That's like buying land in

California after the gold rush. Had the app's creators invested in TikTok Stars and YouTubers, they would have reached a much larger audience.

I hope by now I have clarified that television, its stars, and conventions are all history. That's good for you because you don't have to go through that bottleneck of studio executives and empty suits to get your project made. As long as you produce anything that any set of people find engaging, you're as much of a content producer as Martin Scorsese. Martin himself directed a film for Netflix. And you have Will Smith being a YouTuber. In hindsight, these will all seem like obvious signs for why you should have hopped on the content creation bandwagon.

Many will wish that someone spelled it out for them. Fortunately for you, I am quite literally urging you to get started. Aside from live sports, everything else has gone to the binge environment on streaming platforms. Digital Pay Per View is slowly replacing live sports, and mark my words, as soon as live events are completely migrated to streaming platforms, TV as we have known it will go away. The only thing that will remain is television as a monitor or a screen for the internet streaming services you subscribe to.

What I want you to consider is the fact that you have the opportunity to have the same job title as Will Smith, and all you need is a mobile phone with a camera and the willingness to step up. If this seems like an exciting prospect, carry on reading as I walk you step by step through the process.

! *

Signposts for the Future

I had a friend who asked out a girl he liked, and by some miracle, she agreed to go on a date. Do you know how they say that to the man with a hammer, everything looks like a nail? My friend loved to bake, so he thought the perfect gift would be to bake a cake for her. He stayed up all night baking the perfect cake only to realize later on that the girl was diabetic. Before you do anything, you have to be sure of the demand.

And while we have discussed a lot about the place content creators have in the future, I am talking about a specific type of content creation: subscription video on demand. This means you will be creating content for which you will be paid. And you cannot move forward with this assumption unless you understand the actual demand.

In this chapter, we will cover the current demand for subscription-based streaming services to signpost towards the future. In the year 2020, according to Statista, 882 million people are currently paying for at least one streaming service. Keep in mind that many people pay for at least two subscriptions in not more. Of course, this spells significant revenue. The same source asserts that the industry's revenue currently stands at 51.6 billion dollars. That's 51.6 thousand million dollars annually spent on paid streaming.

This produces a solid foundation for a case that not only is there a future for you in streaming but that there is enough of a market that you can get paid handsomely for your efforts to provide valuable content to your audience. There are many ways to make money within this space; let's discuss a few of them.

Product Placement

Amazon's hit TV show The Boys got a big budget like the rest of Amazon's $100 million per show budgets. But to justify its budget, the show didn't just rely on subscribers. It featured Almond Joy and Fresca as key plot points. The product placements were woven into the story, and one can assume the brands paid a lot of money for the privilege to be advertised in a manner that cannot be skipped. If you are a comedian, you can make a joke where a product is featured in the punchline. As advertisements become more skippable, brands are willing to pay millions for the right shoutout that is packaged in a way the audience doesn't mind consuming.

Licensing Rights

Most TV studios initially licensed their content to Netflix, which made money off of the subscriptions. However, as the studios launched their own platforms, they started pulling content back from Netflix in favor of their own streaming services. You can also initially start by licensing your content to a provider who has a subscriber base and later launching your own streaming service.

Direct Subscriptions

This is the most independent you can get with your content. If you launch your own paid streaming service, you can get paid by viewers who directly subscribe to your content. This sounds hard to do, but in this book, you will learn exactly how easy this is.

!!

Projections That Demand Action

Economists once believed that as we move into the future, the planet's population would exceed three billion people, and everyone would starve to death. Because of that projection, innovators thought long and hard and came up with what we now know as industrial agriculture. As a result, the world's population at 7 billion people is still better fed than what was previously assumed possible. The point here is that projections inform our moves and help us proceed in the right direction.

So in relation to content, what exactly are our projections? By the year 2025, Statista asserts that the paid streaming industry will reach 85.7 billion dollars in revenue. That is 34.1 billion dollars of additional revenue that will be generated within five years from the writing of this book. An earlier projection that we seem to be heading toward quite accurately suggests that 68.2 million households will have a streaming service by 2022.

So what does that mean for you? It depends. If you are already in the Subscription Video On Demand space, you should be terrified because the industry is expanding quicker than you can handle. And if you are a newcomer, this means you have the opportunity to catch millions of eyeballs and carve a niche within this multibillion-dollar industry.

For this, you will need to be great at marketing. While you will bypass executives and empty suits, you can never bypass people. And the best way to grab significant attention and genuine admiration is through authenticity. Algorithms will come and go, and so will platforms, but the attractive nature of authenticity will forever resonate with humans.

What most studios don't have is authenticity. That is why PewDiePie, a human, gets more subscribers than any brand or company channel on YouTube. So lean into your humanness. Remember that while being unpolished would be a disadvantage on TV, those days are history. In the internet space, the more real you are, the more attention you get.

The next thing you have to be a master of is trends. If you are too worried about looking stupid, you effectively disqualify yourself from the race of making money streaming. You need to experiment with hundreds of ideas and trends before one of them sticks or goes viral. You cannot possibly produce that volume if you are too stuck on how you will be judged.

Finally, to be successful in attracting subscribers, you will need to master collaborations. There are those who already have an audience, and if you can give them value, you can be a guest on their podcasts or act in their skits and cross-promote your channel. Even the biggest movies do crossover events to cross-promote their content to two audience pools. That said you have to make sure you have something truly valuable to offer or be prepared to pay creators to be a guest on their show. And when your platform is big enough, that's where you can charge up and comers to be on your show.

Caution – Money Ahead

Before we get into strategy, content creation, and the technology of it all, this is one final chapter priming you for the project you are about to shoulder. I firmly believe that your success depends on how excited you are about something. And I want to hammer home the point that this is not a nice 'what if' fantasy about being popular online; this is your legitimate opportunity to get richer than you probably imagined possible, thanks to being at the right place at the right time.

When I began research for this book back in 2019, the Subscription Video On Demand market was meant to generate 22 billion dollars worldwide. And that got me excited. By the time I write the second draft of this chapter, the industry is already making over 51.6 billion dollars. In other words, the industry has more than doubled in present earnings, which was projected as future market size.

Currently, the market is set to grow in five years by over 43 billion additional dollars in annual revenue. I want to emphasize that this is not a one-time income. This is the amount millions of people are collectively paying into the streaming services every year. So there is serious money ahead. A YouTuber getting five dollars a month is counted in this figure as much as Disney getting paid millions of dollars. I do not know how much money you will make, but I know how much money you can make.

Theoretically, you can make up to 43 million dollars a year for sixty years without creating a new paid TV subscriber. That's what you can make from people who are already willing to pay for content. So I will let your optimism decide what you will make. And I want you to start investing your time in this seriously.

I want you to act like you are about to do a real estate deal. Your content is as much of a legitimate asset as any tangible asset in the real world. So follow these best practices when creating content because you have to keep in mind the money ahead:

Never Sell Your Content Rights

Never ever sell away the rights to your content. Remember to license the rights whenever you put your content on a platform. You never know when you will become a hot commodity and need your content back.

Royalty Is Senior to One-Time or Fixed Payments

When you license content to a paying platform, the owners may try to get you to sign for a fixed payment deal. It is always better to sign a percentage-based compensation structure.

Data Is the Most Important Thing

Your fans are only a borrowed audience if you don't have a way of reaching them. Always keep your number or email visible and encourage correspondence so you have a database of your followers that you can always reach out to if you were to launch a new show or service.

As long as you keep the above three in mind, you will not find yourself on the short end of the stick as far as money is concerned as you move into content creation. Now let's get to a proper strategy so we can build your streaming empire.

STEP THREE

LEARN FROM

THE LEADERS

The Key Lesson From Netflix

As streaming services rise left and right, Netflix will be crowned as the leader that brought in the golden age of Subscription Video On Demand. However, many "leaders" have found themselves firmly placed in the past as newcomers disrupt and take away their market share. Netflix's leadership is pretty much the same that put Blockbuster out of business. And that leadership has proven time and time again to be fit for navigating Netflix through a changing landscape.

The first danger that Netflix faced was that it did not really have any of its own content. Through licensing deals gave the company the right to stream content from other studios, none of it was in perpetuity. In other words, Warner Brothers, Universal, Disney could eventually refuse to renew the deal and leave the platform with no content.

So how did Netflix navigate this obstacle? The company started focusing on original programming as early as day one of shifting to streaming. Now the company is moving towards having 80% of its programming be completely original. Another strategic victory for the leadership of Netflix was when they successfully tapped multiple niches to get devout fans from different sub-genres.

TV shows like Lucifer had a very passionate fanbase, but it wasn't big enough to warrant a TV network to pour money into it. As you know, TV channels make money by airing shows and running ads. And ad revenue incentivizes the number of people watching, not how deeply they are invested. Netflix, on the other hand, gets compensated directly for the content, which means how deeply people fall in love with its content counts.

!'

Netflix started "rescuing" canceled shows by giving them a last chance at producing a closure-giving conclusion to the series after their respective TV networks dropped them. Once Netflix realized how much this pays off, it invested heavily into talk shows and stand up comedy paying Dave Chapelle over a hundred million dollars to get exclusive content. As a result, the platform gained more and more subscribers.

These seem to be different strategies on the surface, but it turns out, Netflix has only been playing a single strategy throughout its existence. The moment Netflix became known for being a platform one can subscribe to for digital content, Netflix had to become something else because anyone can launch such a platform.

Netflix decided to prioritize how much people love content. And staying in line with this strategy, Netflix does not compete with other streaming services. It competes with whatever online activity people love deeply. In a letter to shareholders, Netflix alleged that it sees Fortnite as a bigger threat than HBO or Hulu. If one likes Game of Thrones or another HBO show, Netflix can do little to convince that person not to watch. But at the end of the day, there is only a limited amount of time one can watch a particular show. Netflix can still grab the attention of someone who has watched 80 hours of Game of Thrones. But if someone is invested in Fortnite, he or she is spending that kind of time every week on the game. How Netflix tackles this will be interesting to watch, but the key lesson for you is to prioritize unique, addictive engagement over anything else.

The Key Lesson From Disney

Disney has an iconic brand powered by the global domination of Walt Disney's creative genius that brought us the modern retellings of fairy tales, funny characters like Donald Duck and Mickey Mouse, and live-action content like High School Musical and Hannah Montana.

By all accounts, Disney could have been something you looked back at with rose-tinted glasses and nothing more. But the leadership of Bob Iger propelled the company into heights of success, making it one of the biggest entertainment conglomerates in the world.

Iger was driven by passion and loyalty to the Disney brand, and he dreamed of being a CEO when he was just a manager at one of the Disney-owned companies: ABC broadcasting. When Iger did become the CEO he always wanted to be, he talked some of the most celebrated creative geniuses into selling their companies, characters, and stories to Disney. Under his leadership, Disney acquired Marvel Studios, Pixar, and Star Wars. People he got on board his vision included Steve Jobs, George Lucas, and Stan Lee.

All the while, Bob had his eyes on launching Disney+ a subscription-based streaming platform that would house Disney's entire nostalgia catalog as well as new content acquired by Disney. For him, making a one-time payment of any size was a small price to pay to buy a company that had content he could repeatedly charge for. And that math is the key lesson to learn from Disney.

Suppose you pay a mid-sized YouTuber with a very passionate fan base ten million dollars for exclusive rights to his content; it may seem like a very expensive deal. But if his fanbase converts to subscribers, with only a hundred thousand subscribers, you would start making hundreds of thousands of free money in nine years. And that is the kind of time large corporations can easily afford to wait.

Disney didn't invest as heavily into YouTubers because that is not where Disney's strength lies. Disney's strength was always the iconic characters, and Bob Iger went out and collected more of them. Now it wasn't just Mickey Mouse that you pay Disney for; you also have Iron Man, The Simpsons, and Luke Skywalker. And that is how by leaning into its strength and prioritizing subscription over one-time payments, Disney got to launch Disney+ with incredible success.

So how can you use this lesson in your own platform's success? Take inventory of what your audience truly loves about you and get more of that. If they watch your prank videos, it is time to create a prank network. If you are interested in personal development, it is time to partner with other content creators and get their content on your platform.

Pay the money upfront to get content in perpetuity. If you can pay someone whose audience would pay you, you are golden. All you have to do is create the platform and collect the payment. It really is that simple. The technology aspect of it is not that hard; I own a tech company and understand this. Just getting an app developer on your payroll will lead to you having the platform. This leaves only the content deals as the key work that needs to be done. And the right deals will pay for the right meals. That's what Disney has taught us.

")

The Key Lesson From Amazon Prime

Amazon has a reputation for completely dominating any market or location they enter. Many countries like China and India have their own strategies to hinder Amazon's progress. When governments are afraid of your effectiveness at market domination, you know you are worth studying. In this chapter, we look at the key lesson Amazon teaches us with how it handled Amazon Prime.

Prime TV was coming in after Netflix and Hulu had established themselves. Amazon would never be naive enough to just assume that its product would sell itself. That's the mistake amateurs make. When we launch a product, we assume it is special enough to grab a market share. But just because we feel like it is special does not mean that people see it any differently to hundreds of other businesses and products out there.

I often cite the fact that the first pizza topping introduced to the mass market, Pepperoni, is still the most popular pizza topping in the world almost 70 years later. Why is that the case? Because when something is adopted, people need a very compelling reason to abandon it.

In other words, the people who subscribed to Netflix are owned by Netflix until Netflix messes up. In the meantime, our boy Jeff Bezos has to engineer a service so different from Netflix that it makes a case for people to see it in a category completely separate from Netflix. That's where Amazon Prime leaned into its strength.

"!

People love to shop on Amazon. In particular, they love that Amazon delivers its products in a relatively short period. So Amazon Prime doubles down on that and provides same day and next day deliveries. Yes, the service wasn't marketed as a streaming service but as a service to speed up your shopping. For less than fifteen dollars, getting your orders at your doorstep in a few hours sounds amazing, and Prime Video is an add on. Yes, the streaming service is a free add on to getting your deliveries the next day. This is known as bundling.

Amazon bundled the most in-demand aspect of their existing business with its streaming service to grab a market share. What does this teach us? Firstly, you have to rely on your strength as every giant we have looked at in this section has. More specifically, you have to be open to bundling what people really need from you with what you really want to sell people. Think about how fairy tales handle kids. Kids don't want to learn lessons; they want a story. But in a fairytale, they get the whole bundle: a story with a moral at the end.

So use a similar funnel strategy to capture the audience for your streaming service. If you are an artist, bundle exclusive art deliveries with your subscription video on demand. Steven Crowder, a right-wing internet talk show host, launched the Mug Club, which involved people subscribing to the club to get his merchandise and getting access to his daily show as opposed to his weekly YouTube show. If you are a consultant, you can bundle frequent live-calls with subscriptions to your video vault. The point of this chapter is to give you the principle; how you materialize it into strategy is up to you.

The Key Lesson From Masterclass

If you are interested in cooking, you can learn from Gordon Ramsay; if you are interested in singing, you can learn from Christina Aguilera. And if you are interested in basketball, Stephen Curry is at your service. When it comes to learning from celebrities, the sky's the limit thanks to Masterclass. The company launched with less than ten celebrities on board and now has hundreds of celebrated authors, entertainers, CEOs, and industry leaders on board. The brand became the Netflix of personal development. But it understood how important it was to market personal development in a way that appeals to the masses. For this, they adopted celebrities.

The lesson from Masterclass is not that you must go out and invest in celebrities you cannot afford. The lesson is in borrowing audiences. In other words, if Masterclass's founders tried to get your attention with "hey, we can teach you stuff," you would have been like, "yeah, I can learn stuff on YouTube." When it comes to learning and self-education, you are competing with free content. That is not exactly an easy battle to win.

But the founders of Masterclass got celebrities to say, "I will teach you my craft." And even though none of the lessons are thorough enough to make you a master, that kind of marketing worked with each celebrity's core fanbase. Multiply that with hundreds of celebrities, and the platform has millions of subscribers.

The key lesson for you is not that you should borrow Will Smith's audience but that you can borrow an audience. If someone has ten dedicated viewers, you can be a guest on their podcast, and you have ten potential subscribers for your service. You can do this hundreds of times across any number of days. That said, your appearances will not automatically convert everyone to your platform. That is why you have to understand a few principles.

Firstly, there must be an incentive for people to get interested in your service. I often say that a free trial is the new thank you. You have to allow risk-free entrance into your funnel. You have to also cater to their needs. If you show up on the channel of someone who people follow just for the flashes of her cleavage, and you go there with your cleavage as a forty-year-old man, I doubt that you will convert a lot of her followers to your subscribers. But if you go on a business podcast and drop some real knowledge and follow it up with an offer to learn from you through the paid subscription, you will pump up the conversion numbers.

So to use this strategy, your first step is to count the key people you can collaborate with but also make sure their audience wants what you have to offer. Then appear on their podcast or channel and offer a limited-time incentive to sign up. And if you do those steps right, you will have more paying subscribers than you'll know what to do with.

The Wide-Open Niches

Imagine a man getting down on one knee, opening a ring box with an expectant smile, and saying the magic words, "will you marry me?" There's a pause, and then he receives a slap across his face. "How dare you! You already know I'm married."

That's what happens metaphorically to those who go after customers who are already spoken for. Don't try to compete in niches that have already been saturated. If you read the book so far and kept having the thought that you aren't a movie studio owner, that's good because there are already enough streaming services for streaming movies and tv series. Your subscription video-on-demand service has to be in a space that is not yet completely saturated.

Remember that the earlier you are, the less you need to do to capture an audience. So make the battle easier for yourself by getting into a niche that has less competition.

Area-Specific Personal Development.

Masterclass has proven that it is possible to generate millions of dollars by monetizing personal development. But as the platform tries to be everything to everyone, it leaves behind much to be desired in terms of depth.

If you are a business consultant, you can start an in-depth business academy online. I have done this with ATS Business University. If you are a farmer, produce a streaming service that teaches people how to farm. Teach people how to build a home garden and teach them how to plant across acres of land. Go as deep as possible.

Personality-Specific Reality TV.

If there is one thing that is evident, it is that reality stars have not monetized themselves well online. Keeping Up With The Kardashians lasted more than 19 seasons, but the same girls are putting their life up for free viewing when it comes to social media. WWE did it well with the WWE Network, where every bit of their stars' lives is monetized. You have older stars hosting podcasts, reality TV shows with other stars, and finally, you have the actual wrestling. When the time comes, WWE is best positioned to launch a subscription video-on-demand service.

If you are a personality that people love, you can build an audience online and turn your whole life into the content. You can host a podcast, do sketch comedy, have a monologue show, and have a camera follow you in different situations. You don't need to be in front of the camera; you can adopt the same formula with a current micro-celebrity and take a cut of the profit.

The more specific you get, the more niches open up. Comedy-only networks have been spoken for, and so are martial-arts related niches. But everything else is wide open— Romance network, Action Network, whichever genre of content you like you can double-down on. But my advice is to pick either the area-specific personal development or personality-specific reality TV because both of those have extremely low start-up costs, and you can make a lot of money by being among the first to pull it off.

STEP FOUR

AVOID THESE

MISTAKES

Not Protecting Your Content

Copyright has become an opinion. Only if you have high-powered lawyers and the right tracking mechanism can you track down pirates who are stealing your content and repurposing it for their own means? Many content creators don't really realize the value of their own content.

Remember that Joe Rogan got a $100 million deal for his content library. After that, every content creator is supposed to look at their own content libraries as worth millions of dollars. How accessible would you make a vault with your hundred million dollars in it?

You would not comfort yourself with ideas of recovery; you would be very adamant about preventing theft in the first place. Do you know that anything you put on YouTube can be stolen? There are different types of stealing; firstly, you can just have your content downloaded re-uploaded on another channel where the pirate makes money from showing ads on your content. There's also a more nefarious way of stealing where someone can take valuable information and deliver it on a new video without giving you credit. Your song lyrics, your informational content, and your jokes are all vulnerable to this type of stealing.

How to Use SVOD As a Solution.

Remember that those pirating content are just lazy people who don't want to do the work. So when you place the majority of your content behind a paywall, they just move to another free content creator. This way, your Subscription Video On Demand platform acts as a filter for those who want to steal content and re-upload it to show ads.

Of course, this does not mean that you hide all your content behind a paywall. Even Netflix has a free YouTube account to post trailers and best clips. This will act as a promotional tool for your actual service. When this content is stolen and distributed, your actual service becomes more popular. In other words, you don't exactly mind this type of content getting pirated.

Start by dividing your content library into "outreach content" and "flagship content." Outreach content is meant to be your calling card to those who aren't introduced to you yet. This is the beginning of the funnel. This is what gets people in the door. Flagship content is what people will pay for. This is content they cannot possibly get anywhere. The exclusivity of this content is what makes it special. Consequently, you cannot let this content get pirated, so it has to be behind a paywall.

Make sure to promote your subscription video-on-demand service left to right and center in your promotional content. You can have a watermark of the website address where people can subscribe. You can plug the service in the video. Use whatever you can to shoutout your service and leave the outreach content for free consumption. If it gets stolen, it will only promote your paid service. If it doesn't get stolen, at least your YouTube and other free-viewing audience will get to learn about your paid service.

#*

Monetizing Wrong

One of the biggest mistakes millionaires make is monetizing their content the wrong way. As a result, for every million dollars they can make, they end up making a hundred dollars. Yes, that's how bad the math is on some of the most popular content monetization tools out there.

Let's take, for instance, YouTube's Ad network. You make money if someone sits through the ad. That means someone who came to pay attention to you has to be distracted enough for you to barely make a dollar. With the advent of AdSense and similar programs, you are left with an even smaller pool of people to show ads to.

As a result, you are left with fewer people seeing the ads, even fewer skipping the ads, and even worse, you not having any control over the kind of ads that run over your content.

If you are named John Doe, and you put out content, I can specifically target ads saying "John Doe sucks" and have them roll over your content. The advertisers have all the power; creators have very little. So for this trade-off, what do you earn? You can earn up to four thousand dollars by uploading content twice a week if you have around sixty-thousand subscribers.

That sounds like a substantial amount of money till you realize that by only half of them signing up for your $1/month service, you could be making thirty thousand dollars without ever having to worry about copyright strikes, demonetization, and a host of other problems associated with being a content creator for youTube.

Before we move to the next monetization strategy, let's take a break and talk about our sponsor NordVPN. Just kidding, we aren't paid by them but hasn't that happened in videos you watch? You are all invested in a topic only for the creator to stop and shoutout a product you are not even interested in. That's the second most popular way of making money as a creator online. Of course, this is bad for your audience retention as you are making money by annoying, interrupting, and disrupting your audience. That does not get you very far; as far as rapport is concerned.

The third monetization strategy is to sell your shirts and other merchandise. This is a very good strategy because you are making more of the money. You put in a dollar to get a mug and sell it for nine; hooray, you made nine dollars in profit. But here's where I think most creators don't go far enough. Why stop at selling a one-dollar-cost product for ten dollars? Why not have a $0 product that you can sell for ten dollars every month on repeat forever?

But Antonio, what sort of product is that? That's a subscription video on demand! Why sell physical products when you can film digital content and sell subscriptions to your loyal followers. That's the best monetization strategy, and that's what will make you a millionaire in ten times shorter periods than just relying on Google ads that show up before your YouTube videos.

Relying On a Third-Party Interface

It costs money to host content and to maintain the technology that delivers content. So none of these platforms that house your material for free are really free. They are using you to benefit themselves. And while that might be obvious in an ad-share arrangement where you can see that the network takes fifty percent of the revenue, it is much more sinister in how the platforms are engineered.

Years ago, Ticketmaster came out as this seemingly benevolent platform where you could easily side-step the event companies and sell tickets to your customers. Comedians hopped on this opportunity to promote their shows and sell tickets. However, they realized it too late that the platform was not just taking the cut of the tickets but also using each comedian's audience to prop up other comedians.

When you don't use your own interface, you give power to another platform. The interface is designed to promote other creators. When someone books a show on Ticketmaster, even before they pay for the tickets they intend to buy, they see similar show suggestions. Yes, the platform gives one an opportunity to change their mind about the performer who sent them on the platform in the first place.

If you think that's unfair, look at what YouTube does. Let's suppose you are a farmer who is teaching how gardening and agriculture works. Youtube's algorithm will find the videos that match as closely as possible with your content and suggest those clips to your subscribers on their homepage.

The homepage is not the same as the subscription feed. So when someone goes on Youtube.com, they don't see the content they have subscribed to; they see content similar to what they have watched. See, Youtube has more power if someone is interested in a thousand of their creators. On the other hand, if too many people are on the platform for just one creator, that creator can leave and take the audience with him. And that would be very, very bad for YouTube.

So right there, you have a conflict of interest. It is a conflict of interest that is present in all third-party interfaces that are free to use. As long as the platform relies on creators to make money, it will keep funneling your audience to your competition. Even if you are the first in a niche, Youtube's creator studio will show your competition that your niche is popping. As a result, the sub-category will get swarmed by new content, and it will all be suggested to the audience you earned. On a third-party interface, your audience is a borrowed audience. The solution is to play their game: you funnel the audience YouTube gives you to your platform just like they funnel your audience to other YouTube creators. That is the only way to make this a win-win.

All in all, you have to be very cautious as there is no free lunch in the world of streaming. Remember that your audience is always being funneled by a third-party interface to different creators because the platform wants to diversify your audience's interest, so they rely on the platform more than on you. Your best possible solution to this is to funnel the audience to an interface you own so you have better control over the audience's experience.

##

Not Branding Your Content

This mistake is not too costly in the short term, which leads to more people making it. Collectively, many content creators have lost millions of dollars because they've failed to brand their content. The deal Spotify made with Joe Rogan wasn't just because Rogan had an audience; many YouTubers have more people following them than Rogan's channel. But Rogan was corporate-ready with his branding, which was consistent across multiple platforms.

When creators get confined to one platform, they get complacent in branding their content according to what works for the platform. That is why you will see thumbnails that seem like clones of each other. Here's the problem with that: if your content looks just like someone else's content, you don't have a distinct identity strong enough to monetize.

You have to understand how corporations pay creators. The executive who loves your content would have to go to his senior and show your content. And if it is not branded distinctly, the executive will be asked to single out and start approaching others whose content looks similar. Yes, your content gets price-shopped when you don't have the right branding.

That is why I recommend that you get your content on multiple platforms and house the most valuable content on your own platform. That way, you will get to brand the content as you see fit and not have to worry about having to make your thumbnails look a certain way.

At this point, you may be wondering whether you can just have your own brand housed on YouTube. Of course, you can, but the problem is that as soon as your content starts working, other YouTubers will start doing exactly what you are doing, and your brand will get copied so many times over, even you won't know who the original one is.

So the issue is not just that YouTube or other platforms restrict the ways in which you can brand your content but also that within those boundaries, when you do create a truly distinct brand, others copy it, and it no longer is unique. When it comes to making your content player be a certain color, the loading animation be a specific way, good luck getting any branding other than that of YouTube or Facebook. Facebook has to rub the blue and white in people's faces; the platform doesn't care if your brand colors are pink and peach, which do not go well with blue at all. You have to reign in your brand to match the platform.

In conclusion, branding problems are yet another class of issues that arises in part because creators don't have their own platforms. As a result, they are confined to adjusting their brand colors to match the content player. Furthermore, any unique elements they bring to open platforms are at risk of getting copied. Be wise like Rogan, and create a brand that stays consistent across multiple platforms, and just like he has had his website since day one, always have your own platform.

Letting Go of Data

In the world of content creation, there is no tragedy greater than that of missing out on the data pie. Data is the oil of the future. Countries like China and our own United States have spent billions of dollars to gather data. Earlier, I mentioned Ticketmaster. The entire company was propped up purely by data. Suppose you are a rapper setting up a concert in a very specific area. Anyone who buys a ticket through Ticketmaster gives the company their phone number, email, and name. The company already knows they love rap. Now the company can promote the next rap show to your audience.

Furthermore, if you are to do a show and not cut Ticketmaster in, you cannot reach your own audience because you don't have their email address. That's what platforms do. How many of your followers' emails do you know? If you have one million followers and Instagram decides they should see ads instead of your posts, you cannot reach your own followers anymore.

If you migrate to a different platform, you will not be able to post and let a hundred percent of your audience know. So what's the solution? Start collecting data at the earliest stages.

I have my personal mobile number listed on my page. Anyone can drop me a text. As a result, I get my most engaged audience's contact information. When people sign up to my platform, they give their email address during the process. And here's where we come back to the importance of having your own platform.

When someone subscribes to your channel on YouTube, they don't give you their email address. They let YouTube know that they like your content. Youtube can then show them other creators who make similar content. So, where is your interest in all this? Nowhere. On the other hand, if you have your own platform, you don't just get their contact data but also know which user is engaged to what degree. That way, you can curate offers according to people's interest levels.

The data is infinitely valuable, and companies have paid millions of dollars for rights of access. One reason why this is the case is that data helps one improve. The analytics you get from YouTube are biased to make you focused more on helping the platform. The data that is shown by Youtube forces you to serve YouTube.

So funnel your audience to your own platform and make sure it has data analytics built into it. Start collecting sign-ups and getting email addresses and mobile numbers. This will come in handy when you move to new platforms. You want to be able to reach your audience directly whenever there is a need. Furthermore, you want to learn specific information that helps you improve your performance towards your own goals, not the goals that YouTube wants you to focus on. And for that, you will need intelligent, unfiltered analytics. So not only do I recommend that you launch your own Netflix but that you make sure it has sufficient data monitoring tools that help inform your strategy.

Lack of Content Management

Imagine Netflix with all the shows that ever came out coming out all at once. The platform would flop so bad it would be a spectacle of the century. Tiger King, The Last Dance, House of Cards, Money Heist, and many more shows were all hits, but they were never all hit at the same time. Attention needs to be carefully walked across different streams of content. And for that, a platform needs proper content management.

Many content creators are not able to plan farther than a few months precisely because YouTube and other platforms are very restrictive in how much content management can be done. Up until the third quarter of 2020, Instagram did not allow scheduling of posts. One had to use third-party software to schedule posts, and if Instagram noticed scheduled activity, your whole page would be taken away.

Without content management, you do not have the ability to scale content or to curate your audience's attention through different aspects of your programming. That means you are only confined to being a portion of what they view through the day.

With my platform, I can be in my audience's ear for four hours every day, but the way it works on Youtube is that the moment someone watches a twenty-minute long video of yours, YouTube suggests twenty more videos of which probably three are yours. By YouTube taking the helm of the users' experience, they are left with fewer and fewer opportunities to connect with you more deeply.

Make Your Content Plan On Paper.

Paper is the least restrictive place to schedule your posts and plan your content. When you start doing the planning on YouTube, you restrict yourself to the space allowed by the platform and the timeframe within which you can schedule. That is why you should plan on paper then find the platforms that match your content plan.

You will have the most freedom in content management on your own platform. That makes for yet another compelling reason as to why you should have your own subscription video-on-demand platform. You will be able to plan seasons of content, best short clips, times of releases, and even releases that go directly to customers' inboxes if you move away from free video-sharing platforms and establish your own Netflix.

When you start managing your own release schedule, you start creating your own economy. You can chart off-seasons and high-income peaks in your earnings across time. Doesn't that sound better than just publishing content on YouTube day in and day out while making a few cents every thousand views or so.

All in all, bad content management will lead to a small content-creation operation that relies entirely on big tech companies. If you take control of your own content management, you will be able to take a vacation for most of the year while the schedule you set continues to make money for you by rolling out new releases every single day.

$*

Lack of Video Control

One of the most annoying things about YouTube is that you cannot really minimize it and listen to music in the background. The moment you minimize the app, it pauses the video. The number of money creators would make if people could simply listen to audio with a minimized YouTube is insane. Yet the platform will simply not allow it because it needs to show the advertisers that all users are watching the ads and not simply listening to them.

This is not the first time that the platform places the interests of the advertisers far above the interests of the individual content creators. If you own your own platform, however, you decide the lengths of video, how the video plays out, and how many videos you can publish. A lack of these restrictions will allow you to scale your income.

Right now, you can only stream one video at a time. So if you are a network of five or more creators and you plan to do a simultaneous stream, only one feed would get access to the live feature. That is why you need to have your own platform. You don't want to be asking the question of 'what can we do?' from within the lens of 'what does YouTube allow us to do?'

Let's look at some of the streaming giants. Netflix became popular because of its binge-friendly environment. It released all episodes of every season at one time. However, it became apparent to the Netflix team that it really takes weekly releases to get people talking about certain shows. As a result, the service switched the release schedule for some of its shows.

Right now, the platform that popularized the term "binge-watching" has series that release on a weekly episode schedule. That's because Netflix can do that. That's the freedom you have on your own platform. You can release a five hundred episode show and have it play in order. Do that on YouTube, and episode 45 will be suggested after Episode 2.

The Key Controls That Matter.

When it comes to controlling your content, you want to control two main aspects: the length of the videos and the volume of the content.

Length of Video.

As more and more people open up to long-form content, it is becoming increasingly popular to spend a day with your favorite YouTuber. With your own platform, you have the freedom to truly expand how long your videos are.

The Volume of Content.

You want to give people as much content as they need to fall in love with you. That isn't really possible with YouTube because, after a certain amount of uploads, you hit a wall where you get diminishing returns because the algorithm starts punishing you and funneling away your audience to other creators.

So it is of the utmost importance that you build these two controls into your very own subscription video-on-demand platform. And with complete ownership, you publish the volume and the length required to build an unbreakable bond with your audience.

Shoehorning Geographically

This is the final mistake most content creators make. You may have noticed YouTubers often engaged in story-time or other rants, and they namedrop their local markets. Why is that? Because they are geographically shoehorned by the platform. It turns out that YouTube tracks who watches our content and suggests your content to more people who are similar. This is a double-edged sword. On the one side, this is great because it helps more people learn about you. But it is also bad because when suggesting your content to a similar audience, YouTube often shows it to people who live in the same area.

This hinders your global access as more and more people in close vicinity to each other find out about you. If you have your own platform, you can have a truly global reach as your campaigns can funnel people from all over the world.

Your reach goes as far as your marketing can go. And with that, you have the opportunity to build a global brand. At this point, you might be wondering why you can't just do a global marketing campaign for your Youtube channel. And the answer is pretty simple: because you will just be earning subscribers for your competition.

As you introduce more and more people to your channel, you insert them into Youtube's funnel. The issue with YouTube is that it doesn't funnel the audience in your favor. IT only moves the audience away from you and towards similar creators. As mentioned elsewhere in this book, it is in YouTube's interest that your audience is invested in other creators so that YouTube can retain them even when you move away from the platform.

So you tell me: does It seem like a wise decision to spend your own money and time to grab a global audience only to bring them to YouTube? It costs money to grab attention, and that is why you should not take the audience you earned anywhere but to your own platform. Netflix has a Youtube channel. That means Netflix does not mind promoting itself on Youtube, so you visit Netflix.com and subscribe. But have you ever seen Netflix promote its YouTube channel on any other platform?

You will never find an ad for the company's Youtube channel on Netflix.com because the audience that Netflix has earned it wants to keep on the platform. That is how Netflix has built a truly global brand. To this day, Netflix's youtube channels are not as global. There are separate channels on YouTube for Netflix India and Netflix Espanol, for example. If that doesn't show that YouTube geographically limits channels, I don't know what does. My point is that if Netflix can't have a global audience on YouTube, you can't either. Get rid of the illusion that Youtube is global and lay the foundation for your own platform, which you will make truly global by marketing to different countries and peoples just like described in this book. And if you are already thinking about marketing, then you're ready for the next section.

STEP FIVE

FIND YOUR

AUDIENCE

$$

Video is Rapport

Have you ever shown someone the guy or the girl you like only to notice by their expression that they can't see what's so attractive? If you've been in such a situation, you know what the go-to phrase is: "he's cuter in person, or she's prettier in real life. Why is it that some people seem more attractive in a person? It is because attraction lies in movement. It is in motion that one can see the unique movement of features, the creases that come with smiles, the quality of sound.

No one ever builds rapport with a still. That leads me to believe that video is the foundation of rapport. This has very serious implications for marketing. What it means is that every video you make is a clone of you. By dispensing hundreds of thousands of clones into the cybersphere, you are building authentic relationships with millions of people.

The result of this is a bit creepy because you start to form friendships, not just a following. Hundreds of thousands of people have mentally built a relationship with you and feel like they know you because they are interacting with a clone of you.

Our brains are not prepared for this kind of advancement. But getting a handle on video technology, we have the opportunity to scale friendships. You can give the same relatable experience to a hundred million people provided you reach that many people.

In marketing your platform, you will need to create content from a place of empathy. The idea is to create content so narrowly targeted at your niche that every individual listening believes that you are a personal friend giving direct advice and sharing stories one-on-one. As you become a friend to hundreds of people, simply ask them to share your content with others because that's what friends do. Soon your friends will be getting your new friends. And once you have a network large enough, ask your friends to support you by signing up for your own platform, which will be a special thing just for your tribe.

This is simple to do but do not confuse that with easy. At the end of the day, you will have to cultivate a genuine relationship with people over video. Video is rapport, but that also means video exposes fake rapport. If you try to fake a relationship with your viewers, they will be able to tell instantly. People are smart, and it is no longer the times where lies could fly.

All in all, video is an advancement in technology that our brains have not fully grasped. As a result, we form a one-way relationship with the characters we see. You can use this and form genuine connections with your audience and give them calls to action like joining your streaming service or further promoting your videos among their friends. Celebrities, influencers, and video creators use this strategy every single day. Now it is with your reach as well. Use it carefully and for the good of yourself as well as your audience.

Video and Social Media Isolation

The world of social media is a lonely one. While it looks like everyone is connected to everyone else, it is, in fact, the case that everyone is keeping tabs on everyone. Platforms like Instagram and Facebook are meant to help you keep tabs on your friends. As a result, the engagement comes in the form of signals like past likes and comments but never turns into the kind of conversations you would have with a friend.

So what do people do in a situation of super-exposed loneliness? They turn to friends on video. As time passes, they start sitting in on conversations happening on podcasts and start sharing laughs, learning about inside jokes, and so on. The consequence of this is a potential one-way friendship.

When you are launching a platform, you are in the business of creating such relationships. What happens when people visit friends abroad? They spend their time and money to spend some time with people they consider friends. Once you become a friend to your followers, of course, they will travel to your platform and subscribe to be even closer to you. That's the impact of befriending your audience. And that is not possible with word posts or pictures; that is possible only with video.

Video is such a close imitation of reality that it creates a whole world in which your audience gets to step in and understand who you are and what they are to you. This kind of authenticity, compassion, and empathy never translate across other forms of online media communications.

That is why you should understand that there is not even a question of whether or not you will use video marketing. You have no choice but to use video to build the kind of connection that is required between you and your audience.

The first step is to know your audience and know what they crave from a relationship with you. Many creators convey a sense of love, others give affirmations, and there are those who share jokes. No one emotion is right or wrong to convey. As long as you know that your audience craves it and you can genuinely deliver it, go make a monopoly on that emotion.

The next step is to start getting engagement by giving smaller calls to action to your audience. You can tell them to comment related to the video, or you can ask them to share the videos. The effectiveness of this call to action will give you feedback regarding the level of rapport you have with your audience. If at any point, more than fifty percent of the people start following your recommendations, you have built one of the strongest rapports on the platform and can safely funnel the audience to your own subscription video-on-demand platform.

It is worth noting that you should be cautious of faking a relationship with your audience. Inauthenticity shines through, and if you are faking what you pretend to feel towards your audience, you are building a house of cards that will come crashing down; Never let go of authenticity and integrity as you build your empire because that is the only way to ensure longevity.

Learn From the Big Boys

Traveling would be the hardest thing to do if every single traveler had to invent his own ship. That is why we should learn to avoid the tendency to reinvent the wheel and learn to stand on the shoulders of giants like Netflix. The world of streaming has come a long way since there was only one platform that would stream content, and that platform gave a free trial. With more people getting familiar with paying for streaming, it becomes easier to make money by providing content online.

But at the same time, enough competition has risen that viewers have become trigger happy with their cancellation of services. So in this chapter, I will cover the general methods followed by all major streaming platforms to capture a significant market share.

Always Rely on Your Strength.

Remember how we looked at the case study of Disney and found out that the company was relying on its collection of beloved characters to generate a subscriber base? What did they do to expand their market share? They grabbed the rights to more beloved characters. Now, look at Amazon Prime. What is Amazon's strength? A strong product delivery network. And how did Prime TV get marketed? As a free add-on to Amazon Prime, which is a quick delivery service. Both Amazon and Disney seem to be employing completely different strategies, yet the underlying principle is the same: double down on your strength.

Be First or Be Different.

  Remember that the first one to the market has the pick of the audience, and once he or she owns the audience, it is nearly impossible to take that audience away. That said, you don't need to be Netflix to be first. You can be first within your niche. And if you are not first, you have to be different enough to get noticed. In the absence of either of these, you do not have a fair shot at capturing the market and should excuse yourself till you come up with a different content or market segment idea.

Do Not Be Afraid to Look Stupid.

  After Netflix got the market leadership position, anyone trying to take its market share was ridiculed and told that it was a fool's errand, yet enough executives went at a problem that, as of today, the leadership of the subscription video-on-demand market is uncertain. We do not know whether HBO Max or Disney Plus will take over Netflix. And that would not be the case if Disney's Bob Iger or Warner Brothers' CEO were afraid of people's judgment.

  All in all, giant platforms have specific lessons and opportunities for us, and it is worth exploring each one to come up with an action plan that makes sense and helps you create your own successful subscription video-on-demand platform. The common lessons from some of the most celebrated platforms dictate that one relies on his or her strength, is first or is different, and must stop being afraid of looking stupid. Now let's look at what major open platforms present in terms of opportunities.

How to Market Your Platform Using Facebook

Facebook is home to a barrage of videos being uploaded at a rate of four billion per day. This shows the capacity of the platform to take your content and present it to a large enough audience. After all, literally half the world is on Facebook. But you cannot just post any video on Facebook and make the most of it. You have to follow what works for the platform.

One way to find out what works on the platform is to go by the traditional route of trial and error. This leads to a lot of disappointment, frustration, and time lost. Time isn't the only thing you lose. There is quite a real chance you may lose your enthusiasm halfway through. And the loss of enthusiasm is the deadliest thing to a dream. The other way to find out what works on a platform is to follow someone who has figured it out.

Fortunately for you, I have successfully used the platform to develop my own audience. A significant portion of my Facebook audience has converted to my subscription-based video content service. So what is my secret of marketing with video on Facebook? SSP.

SSP stands for Smart, Shareable, and practical. Your content has to pass through this checklist to be the ideal material for Facebook. The platform is designed to propagate content. If you share something that is practical, people will tag their friends in the comments of the video. If your content is smart, people will feel nice sharing it. And of course, if the content is sharable, it has the potential to go viral.

A word of caution, however, you don't want to confuse smart content with trying to look smart. The last thing you need to do is cultivate an air of pretentiousness. Remember that in the absence of everything else, cling to authenticity. The key benefit of video marketing is that it allows you to gain trust. And the moment you try to put on fake airs about yourself, you lose trust. And that is not good at all.

What Makes Content SSP?

The content becomes smart, shareable, and practical when you ask yourself, "Is this content I would interrupt my busiest friends to show?" This one question can keep you from putting out bad content. If your content is always good enough to warrant interrupting busy friends, it has a higher chance of getting shared by your audience.

Remember that different people find different content to be SSP. What is SSP for Millennials might be trash to baby boomers and vice versa. So the first thing you need to be sure of is who your audience is, to begin with. Once you are clear about your audience, you can proceed to create SSP content and make sure to always plug your streaming service in the video so you can drive traffic to your streaming service. Not everyone will become an instant convert, but enough people will convert and then tell their friends to give you the beginnings of your own Netflix.

How to Market Your Platform Using Instagram

What is Instagram? Instagram is an opportunity to have a branded experience. Everyone on Instagram is a brand. So when you are marketing your platform on Instagram, you have to be a visually appealing brand. People on Instagram are not there to read books posted as images; they want to interact with you. So use Instagram as a hybrid of TV and magazine.

IGTV and Instagram Video.

As you may have noticed, Instagram is not a single platform but a conglomeration of multiple features. You have to treat Instagram videos as a distinct platform. Use the videos to get your audience curious. Share small clips from your shows but do not give enough context for people to understand where the clip is from. This will make them visit your profile, and that's where your link in bio comes into play.

Link in bio is the single link you are allowed to place on a caption permanently. If you post links in video captions, they aren't clickable, but if you place a link in your bio, people are likely to click it upon visiting your profile. Let the small videos be beautiful clips that don't tell the whole story just so people click your profile and, subsequently, your link in bio.

IGTV is long-form content. Let IGTV be the place where you drop free-for-all episodes. Yes, you can release the pilot episode or any episode from the shows on your platform. When people who browse IGTV come across the video, they will watch it at length and want more. That's when they will click your profile and, you guessed it, your link in bio.

Instagram Stories.

Instagram stories are a replacement for real-life interaction. Therefore you will use these to build rapport with your audience. Don't over-prepare your story. This is where you can tell people facts about yourself. I often challenge people to share one fact about themselves every single day for a whole year. When people feel connected to you, they are more likely to invest in you.

Instagram Live.

Live is a feature many social media platforms have added. Do not make the mistake of assuming that it is the same across all platforms. On Instagram, your live is meant for interaction. The interface is straightforward, and you can get questions in real-time from people. Give answers to their questions, get them hyped about what is coming up, and take them behind the scenes.

Instagram Photos.

Finally, you have the flagship feature of Instagram: photos that stay on your Instagram profile. Use photos to create an aura of celebrity. A feed is a perfect place to be your own paparazzi. Whatever image it is that you want to convey, this is the place to build that image.

All in all, Instagram is a robust platform that continues to diversify its features as time passes by. As long as you don't lump all features into a single sludge, you will be able to market your video on demand platform in multiple ways. Any feature rolled out by Instagram is perfectly optimized to market yourself; just ask yourself, "how can I use this to make people click the link in my bio?"

How to Market Your Platform Using Snapchat

Snapchat is a platform where users are prone to have a smaller attention span. Your job is not to fix the attention span of those on Snapchat. Remember, you are on a social media platform to allow people to have fun in the way they want to have fun. That means you are not going to give people seven pages to read on Instagram because people are there to see pictures. So what are people there to do on Snapchat? People are on Snapchat to watch small duration content, and that's exactly what you are going to give them.

Be loud, attention-grabbing, and flamboyant on Snapchat. You do not get to choose how you are going to be when you market. There is a certain way you need to behave in order to catch attention. Celebrities, politicians, businessmen all have to follow the principle of grabbing attention. When you can't grab attention, someone who is less concerned with looking stupid is going to grab their attention and take them off to his or her video platform.

How to Be Attention-Grabbing Without Being Annoying.

Often we become attention-seeking instead of being attention-grabbing. There's a big difference between the two. When you are attention-seeking, you are desperate for attention but don't do anything productive with it. On the other hand, when you are attention-grabbing, you take people's attention then bring them value.

Think of attention like money. People don't mind parting with their money as long as they receive what they find more valuable than the money. People also don't really have control over their attention. So when people steal their attention but give them nothing in return, they are as angry as a person whose wallet got stolen, and he was given nothing in return. On the other hand, when you grab attention but deliver valuable lessons, highly entertaining content, the person feels happy that you got their attention. Think of it like someone who stole ten dollars from you but gave you an iPhone. While you still feel violated, you are kind of glad he stole your ten dollars because you value the iPhone more.

So sit down and make a list of things people value more than their attention. Jonah Berger, in his book contagious, says that people like to get to know about things that they can point others to and look good. So if you can create content that makes your audience look good, you can be as flamboyant and loud on Snapchat as possible, and anyone who gives you attention will be better off for it.

In conclusion, remember that the audience on Snapchat is there to view short clips and pictures that disappear. So use the short timeframe and don't try to reinvent the wheel. Maximize your flamboyance and grab attention in the shortest period possible. As long as you give people what they value more than the attention you got, there will be no goodwill lost, and people will even be happy that you stole their attention.

How to Market Your Platform Using Twitter

Twitter is a place where people value getting an accurate reflection of reality. Remember that in the legacy of Twitter, you have the Arab spring where multiple Arab countries had their revolutions that were broadcast on the platform, and the world participated in moral support. You cannot go to that platform with a fake flamboyance. You have to make your content real, social, and direct.

Real.

When you are marketing your platform on Twitter, you have to make sure you are honest and authentic with your audience. You have to connect with people by being direct and sharing with them the wisdom that they can take to their real lives.

If your platform is a sketch comedy platform, make a funny video that reflects the realities of life. Ii is more likely to go viral. If you have a platform where you teach business and leadership, make a content snippet that gives real-life advice on how to handle a business problem. What you don't want is a clip that has no effect on reality. IF it is not real, Twitter is not interested. It is a platform for citizen journalism and what is useful in the real world is newsworthy for Twitter.

Social.

A huge part of our experience is social. And this is especially true for Twitter. You need to give people the opportunity to look good while they share your content. IF your content is useful, they will share it and look nice in the process. You can make meme-worthy content that people can exercise their wit on. For instance, if you share a screenshot from one of the shows on your subscription platform and the character's expression is sad, someone can share it with the caption "when I realize it is Monday" is social content, the person sharing it has the ability to interject and contribute and in the process look good to his or her social circle.

Direct.

Twitter has a character limit. And that is what has trained its audience to have a decent attention span but to have little to no tolerance for ragged out irrelevant content. And that's true not just for captions but also for the content of the video you are using to market your platform.

So forget about hour-long videos priming the audience about your platform. Make direct announcements as to why the audience you have on Twitter needs to be on your video-on-demand platform. Let them know the free trial offer you have, inform them about the exclusive content and perks of joining you on the other side.

In conclusion, when you are marketing on Twitter, you are marketing to an audience of self-titled journalists. Ask yourself, "Is this newsworthy?" before making any content for Twitter. And as soon as you make the content, find out ways in which you can optimize it for sharing? How can you allow people to share it so that they look good? And finally, cut all the fluff. People on Twitter like to get to the point as soon as possible. Make a strong argument for joining your platform and make it count.

STEP SIX

GET YOUR

OWN NETFLIX

&*

The Common Person Customer

Before you launch your own Netflix, you have to know what the Netflix business model really is. The streaming giant is in the business of killing boredom. And boredom is in an infinite supply across time. You have to understand that boredom is the problem of every individual. We may have preferences towards how we choose to kill boredom. For instance, those with productive preferences binge content that is education. There are those who have harmless preferences like watching comedies. I am not judging anyone. But the point I am making is that your customer is the common person.

There's no such thing as a 'viewer.' Everyone is a viewer of something. Because some streaming companies try to go out in search of a 'viewer' they pick a fight with already established businesses. Fighting over the same customers is a losing battle where you keep lowering your prices and thinning out your margins.

Let me remind you of the earlier example from this book: Pepperoni Pizza introduced after the second world war is still the most popular pizza topping in the world. IF someone already has a viewer, they have the viewer. People stick to what they get used to first. You are creating your own Netflix, but you are not competing with Netflix. You are modeling Netflix for a market of your choosing.

In the next chapter, we will get deeper into Niche selection, but for now, I want you to understand that everyone consumes something, everyone has a credit card, and paying to access a streaming service has been normalized for everyone. So when it comes to finding paying customers for your own Netflix, it is open season on everyone in the developed world.

What It Means for You That Netflix Is Normalized.

You Don't Have to Explain Your Service to Anyone.

Gone are the days when you would have to explain what a paid streaming platform is. You don't have to even tell people why they can't download content after paying for it. There are no objections regarding the minutiae of streaming services that you need to answer because everyone knows how the market is.

Everyone Knows What the Nature of the Transaction Is.

At some point in history, if someone subscribed to a free trial and got charged after forgetting to cancel, he or she would be furious. Nowadays, everyone knows how these transactions work. You don't have customers who are disappointed when the free trial leads to a paid transaction. They understand that their initial access is a trial. And that's all thanks to Netflix making it the new normal.

People Are More Willing to Pay to Stream.

Just like Michael Jordan made basketball global and Connor McGregor made UFC international, Netflix made paying to stream normal. Moreover, this spawned so many streaming services in the wake of Netflix that billions were collectively spent in advertising, convincing millions of users to pay for streaming services. You did not spend a cent, yet most of the global population is already primed to pay for subscriptions to streaming services. It's time to take advantage of that.

The Ultimate Niche Selection Guide

In the previous chapter, you learned about how everyone is in the market for a streaming service. But if you try to be everything to everyone, you will end up like Quibi, which lost three-quarters of a million dollars marketing a platform no one wanted. You have to pick the right niche. There are multiple ways you can go about selecting a niche, but before we discuss any, I need to introduce a case study that will help broaden your mind regarding the possibilities with niches.

Gaia: The Netflix for Conspiracy Theories.

It may be slightly unfair to label Gaia as the Netflix for conspiracy theories, but it wouldn't be entirely inaccurate. The streaming service hosts hours of podcast-tier content on subjects that no one in the mainstream media acknowledges.

In other words, the platform went for those who other platforms don't even care about. If you want hours of content on how the government is hiding aliens and commentary on how we are plugged into the Matrix, Gaia is the place for you.

If you didn't already learn that this platform exists, you wouldn't believe it was even a viable business model. Try pitching this idea to your friends without telling them Gaia exists. I already know what they'll probably say "conspiracy junkies don't pay for stuff, they don't trust anybody." "How many conspiracy theory believers are there, come on. And how many of them watch stuff all day?" and so on.

Since Anything Is Possible With Niche Selection, You Can Go in One of Two Ways.

Go With Your Passion.

If you feel very strongly about something and are one in a billion who is so passionate about it, there are at least seven thousand people who are just as passionate. If you convert even ten percent of them to paid subscribers, you would be making over six thousand dollars a month charging less than ten dollars.

This method is a roll of the dice because you don't know the market size for the niche, but it will still make you a sustainable income, and you will be producing content about something you are truly passionate about. Go with your passion and then find the people who share it.

Discover the Hidden Gem Niche.

This method gives you more of the content platform role, and you will likely not be the bigger draw in terms of your own content. For this, you will first spot popular youtube niches and convince the personalities behind these channels to come to your platform and convert their subscribers into paying customers. Even though this method is going to require you to cut people in on the revenue, you will have much more momentum from collaborative marketing (explained later in the book).

Hidden gem niches are easy to find on YouTube because you just have to scroll through the homepage and watch the content you like. Keep clicking on the 'related videos' titles till you come across content creators with views in tens of thousands. These creators are in a niche that is popular enough for youtube but not big enough for Netflix and similar services to get into.

Lower the Risk, Reap the Reward

Sales training has become a multi-billion dollar industry, yet all salespeople are being trained to do is one thing. And all salespeople have to do is one thing: convince customers that a product is worth risking the money for. In such an environment, businesses that do not lose money by giving their product or service for free have decided to shoulder the risk on behalf of the customer.

In content, online education, and Software as a Service (SaaS) industries, you can afford to let someone try out your products and services without actually losing money. On the other hand, a car manufacturer can't do that no matter how low the cost of production of a car. That's because you scale up without taking on the additional cost of production, while physical goods require you to constantly spend more as you make more.

Now that you understand that you have the edge over most businesses because you can afford to make your product free, let's discuss the wisdom in it.

McDonald's doesn't make a huge profit on its burger sales. Its classic burger gives it a few cents on the money you spend to get it. So why does McDonald's continue to use its resources to make the low-priced burgers? Because they are a low-risk entrance into their sales funnel.

If you are familiar with my consulting and education work, you know I am a fan of the sales funnel or the sales process as traditional conglomerates call it. So you go into McDonald's because you don't mind spending a few dollars for a bite. But as soon as you place the order for a burger, what are you asked? "Would you like fries with that?" And that's where McDonald's makes a bulk of its profit. The price of the fries is nowhere near the cost of store-bought potatoes. But McDonald's gets potatoes much cheaper than those in stores because it has farms as direct suppliers.

So what will be your low-risk entry point? A free trial. And the keyword here is trial. And where will you make your profit? When the users don't cancel their subscription and continue to pay. This business model is very powerful because you invest less than McDonald's spends on potatoes and make more than McDonald's does on the order of fries. In other words, if you scale to the numbers of McDonald's, your company would be at a value higher than that of McDonald's.

But let's not get ahead of ourselves. I have a section dedicated to disruption and scaling, but for now, you must remember that you will be giving free trials with the option to cancel any time. In fact, 'cancel any time' is the new thank you. And while you will initially spend time, money, and energy to get 'customers' who aren't paying upfront, that is the norm of the streaming industry, and just like these conglomerates make much more money on the back end, you will make more as long as you do it right.

Have Clarity About Your Revenue Model

While this book is about creating your own Netflix and Netflix has a Subscription Video On Demand model, you have other options of monetization as well. This chapter is about exploring each despite my personal preference for subscription video on demand.

Pay Per View.

This became popular with boxing and other contact sports. Since title fights cost a lot of money to put together, market, and host, the fight organizers created a system that precedes paid online streaming. One could, and in some instances, still can pay for one unit viewership over cable. But most pay per view has shifted to the online space. Now pay per view is no longer confined to boxing and martial arts broadcasting industries. You can go to your Google PlayStore and pay for a view of one of your favorite movies.

Rent the Content.

While Google does give pay-per-view access to some of the content on the Play Store, most of the content is meant to be rented for a limited time period. This initially was Netflix's business model too. You would get DVDs mailed to you, and you would mail them back after watching. Even today, you can rent DVDs via Netflix, but it is a smaller part of their business.

On the other hand, Amazon Prime allows you to rent movies to stream. It also has a subscription video-on-demand model. So hybrids are a possibility as well.

Subscription Video On Demand.

Subscription Video On Demand is a business model I back because it provides a consistent source of income. Do you remember the earlier example of McDonald's lowering its burger's selling price to barely breaking even just to get the customer in the door? Well, the book Sal, Sugar, Fat describes how the combination of salt, sugar, and fat creates a drug-like addictive effect in humans. So not only is McDonald's acquiring the customer for a single transaction that it can use an upsell to make a profit on, but it is also making sure that the customer it has acquired continues to visit and pay.

While that is a great strategy, it does not guarantee that the customer will come every day or even every month. Subscription-based businesses get a consistent stream of income that is pretty much guaranteed. And if there's anything humans love, it is security.

You will put a lot of effort into launching your own streaming platform. And even though it might take only a month of work, it is work I want you to get fruits of for a long time.

That is why I recommend that you get customers to subscribe to your platform and charge them every month for access to your content. This also works well with episodic content as instead of salt, sugar, and fat, you are using continuation and fear of missing out to get the customers committed to your content. That said, the choice is up to you. It is going to be your platform, after all.

You Can't Spell Bad Without Ad

In the previous chapter, we discussed various monetization strategies, and thanks to YouTube, the first thing that comes to many content creators' minds when they hear the word monetization is 'Ads.' Chances are you may have picked this book because you already are a YouTube content creator. Let this chapter be a lesson in why advertising is a bad business model for content providers.

How Ads Began.

The television advertising industry thrived in times when there were very few networks, and almost every product released to the market was a mass-product. The masses saw TV, they had little choice in switching away from Ads to content without ads, and the ads they saw were broadly appealing to them. That is where the term 'soap opera' came from. Soap operas were tv shows that housewives loved. They had the romance, the drama, and the narratives that spoke to a wife at home. And what was often advertised during the breaks? Soap. And that led to the content being named after the ads.

Let this be a lesson in what it means for your content when you advertise. You lose credibility. Even when Hulu finally switches away from ads completely, the name will always be associated with annoying ad breaks.

Today, the consumer of content has the option to switch platforms. In such a position, it is very unwise to insist on ads because you alienate users who don't like to see ads. Furthermore, the whole revenue model is focused on making money from an easily distracted audience. The viewers who love your content so much they would pay for it get ignored, and the viewers who aren't exactly into your content and will click on an ad instead are the ones that make you money.

In such an arrangement, how would you make more money? By appealing to exactly the audience that loves your content less.

Why You Should Switch Away.

Remember that ads are annoying your audience, and many are willing to pay to watch. So why would you rather make a few cents streaming your content to those who aren't willing to pay for it instead of making the whole dollar streaming to those who can and are willing to pay for it?

Aside from the fact that you make more money, you also have the right incentives. To make more money, you have to improve your content, make sure it truly is the best in its category, and make your audience fall in love with it. And those are the right incentives for a business owner.

Let this chapter be a stitch in time that saves nine. Right after we discuss the revenue model, I want to make sure you are clear that advertising is a bad idea. If people want to watch content with ads, then YouTube has perfected that much better than you with a multi-billion dollar backing. It can provide more niche ads than any network and curate the ads to match peoples' interests. And if you are providing what creators already deliver on Youtube, you have little to differentiate yourself with.

Make It Right With the Rights.

There are streaming services that illegally show the same content as Netflix, and instead of charging money, show popup ads. That is a way to make money and spend more than you earn in fines and legal fees. As the value of content goes up, even YouTube content is becoming harder and harder to use. If you have a YouTube video that includes a few minutes of another video even with fair use, Youtube will delete your video if the person who has the rights to the three minutes flags your content. You will have to go to court to get YouTube to reinstate your upload.

If a multibillion-dollar corporation is that cautious about rights, you have to be. So whenever you convince a content creator to produce content for your platform or give rights to the content to you, make sure you follow these best practices.

- Get a written release form or a formal license.

- The release form would either give you ownership of streaming rights or grant you the right to stream in a non-exclusive capacity.

- The license will give you the right to use with conditions.

- Make sure you have the exclusive right to stream content.

- Make sure any licenses to stream are granting you the right to stream in perpetuity.

It is evident that these conditions are not something bigger stars would ever agree to. That is why you have to find the sweet-spot creator. A creator is in a position where he or she can benefit you but isn't big enough to demand terms that are bad for you.

The way to find such creators is by filtering your YouTube search till you find creators who have an average of ten to twenty thousand views on every video he or she uploads. When you find one, you have your potential partner. That creator is in a space where he or she is making some money from YouTube but not nearly enough to be too good to consider your deal. Within such creators, find those who make videos on a weekly basis and convince them to do daily content for you. If they end their weekly videos by shouting out your platform, their passionate subscribers who want content every day and have a fear of missing out will flock to your platform.

Of course, with ten thousand views on a free platform, barely a hundred will start paying you for daily content. But if you do similar deals with multiple creators, you will have a sizable income. This was done on a larger scale by a YouTube channel called Louder With Crowder. Steven Crowder is a Christian Republican content creator who got his streaming rights acquired by a conservative political commentary network, The Blaze.

While I am not aware of the licensing structure, it is clear that it worked because thousands of people have paid The Blaze to watch Crowder's content every day. And every week he shouts out his 'Mug Club,' which is the name of the service. You buy a mug from his shop and get a monthly subscription. You do not receive cups monthly. That's a one-time free gift, and the actual service you pay for is the daily content from Crowder.

Accessibility Bias Brings the Bucks

Which brand of bottled milk do you buy? Regardless of the name that comes to mind, I have a follow-up. What do you think is the biggest marketing advantage of that milk brand? Is it their pasteurizing process? Is it their advertising dollars? No. It is their ability to be on the shelf where you grab it from.

From necessities like soap to optional pleasures like a can of Coca-Cola, corporations' biggest advantage is their availability on shelves where people pick their products from. And that is why Amazon is such a game changer; before its emergence, businesses had to wait for a gatekeeper to allow them access to customers.

With the online space, the roles have flipped. It isn't about you accessing a space where customers can find you. It is about you being accessible wherever customers need you.

And in the world of streaming, almost eighty percent of streaming is done on a mobile phone. Among other unusual places, people stream movies and TV shows on are gaming consoles and TVs. Yes, as internet-delivered content replaces TV, TV has become a screen for surfing the Internet.

Google 4K monitor and see the prices. Then google 4K TV and see the difference. Because so many 4K TVs are in demand, they are much cheaper to produce, whereas 4K monitors are manufactured in much smaller quantities.

Remember that while people are willing to pay to stream your content, you are effectively keeping them from downloading your content. And since they can't download, they have a disadvantage in that they aren't able to enjoy the content in a variety of ways. For example, if someone downloads a YouTube video, he or she can convert it to an MP3 and listen to it on their phone. They can use a USB or Bluetooth to transfer the video to their phone or use a Chrome-cast to watch it on their TV.

You have to allow them access to all those playing features without the extra work of downloading, converting, and transferring. That way, you spin the inability to download into a feature of not having to download. Remember that Spotify became a multi-million dollar music streaming giant despite all the content still being available on YouTube. Why? Because the YouTube app stops playing when you minimize it. On your laptop, YouTube and Spotify aren't really different. But on mobile, YouTube made it inconvenient to listen to music while texting or while playing games.

Only because of one small inconvenience it lost all that market share and led to a rival. I want to make sure that doesn't happen to you. I want to make sure that all the effort you put into acquiring rights, finding the right niche, and getting creators on board or creating original content does not go to waste as a competitor grabs all the market share by providing the same service on a different device. I want you to encompass all devices. I'll teach you how to do that and for now, I just need you to be willing to be everywhere with your platform.

Native Is the New Exclusive

In the previous chapter, you learned how to spot the right content creators and how to get the rights to their content. Let's now discuss creating your own content because, at the end of the day, we are modeling Netflix. Netflix initially got content streaming rights from other studios, but as the service got popular, the studios started pulling their content from it and starting their own streaming services. To make sure this doesn't happen to you, I made sure you don't sign any temporary licensing deals.

However, Netflix, too, can sign perpetual licensing agreements with smaller studios, yet it chooses to create Native content. Why do you think that is? It's because, at some point, you have to pay so much money to get the complete rights to someone's content that it is much more business-smart to produce your own content.

Netflix's CEO is not acting or producing his own content, but his company owns the content. And that's what I want you to do. If you're a creator yourself, you can start by creating your own content featuring yourself, but if being in front of the camera is a total deal-breaker, I don't want to push you to become a presenter.

Peter F Drucker, the father of the MBA, used to say that most people spend their lives trying to be mediocre at something they are bad at instead of becoming excellent at what they are good at. You can have people who are naturally good at podcasting create content that you can own. In such an arrangement, you pay them upfront to create the content. That's the difference between a perpetuity license and complete ownership.

Here's what I want you to consider: If you go to a YouTuber now and convince them to deal with you on a profit-share and you aren't paying them anything, they will want a significant percentage. If you want exclusive rights in a perpetual arrangement, they will want at least fifty percent of the revenue. That may be fair in the beginning, but when you have hundreds of creators bringing their traffic to you, you will still be paying fifty percent of all that to one creator. And it will be a licensing deal even you can't get out of because it is perpetual. Own the content by paying upfront and offer revenue-sharing for up to a month just to incentivize them to send their viewers to your platform.

All in all, remember the difference between licensing and ownership and always prioritize ownership. The cheapest way to own your own content (especially in a podcasting-type genre) is to create it. And the easiest way is to buy its exclusive rights by paying up-front. So you decide whether you prioritize ease or cost-effectiveness. Either way, I implore you to develop your own podcasting and content creation skills if you have even a seedling of potential in the space. But if you don't, I recommend that you develop your content acquisition skills to make up for it and excel in that area. Either way, all is well if you own the content.

Your Own Netflix in a Week

You have arrived at the most important chapter of this book. While the book before this and after this is about the business and the success, this is the technical aspect. If you read only this chapter, you will know how to create your own Netflix. You may be wondering all along, "How do I build the actual platform? I am not a team of coders!" then let me introduce you to clone scripts.

Clone Scripts 101.

How do platforms like Facebook, YouTube, and Netflix work? They are software written in a programming language using a code. This code is then put on a server, and when you type the web address or open the app, you access that code from the user-end. Your android, iOS, or web browser are specialized at reading this code and converting it into everything that you see upon opening the platform. Your clicks are commands that the software is coded to react to in the way that it does. When you click the fullscreen icon, the code makes the video take up the whole screen.

Fortunately, you don't have to learn coding to create all of this; you can simply get a copy of the code. Where do you access the code from? Well, let's look at a simple example. What is the common response to "thank you"? It is "You are welcome." If anyone comes up to you and asks you, "What phrase do people say 'you are welcome' as a reply to?" What would you say? "Thank you." That's because by knowing the result, you can reverse engineer the stimulus.

Well, coders can just as naturally reverse-engineer the script of any Platform. Now what you need is to get yourself the clone script of Netflix. For this, you should Google "Netflix

(*

Clone Script," and you will open yourself up to a whole marketplace of different Clone Scripts. The best part about this is that you cannot copyright code.

That Is because code is like words. While Les Brown can copyright his books, he can't copyright the word hungry just because of how prominent It is in his main message. While copying the code and the visible brand will get you in legal trouble, using a clone script to create your own Netflix with your own branding is fine. That's because every streaming service uses the same code.

So as long as you can get a Netflix clone script and host it on a server (Web Hosting solutions exist and are pretty cheap), you will be able to have your own Netflix. For legal reasons, I recommend that you change the appearance. And you can get the customization at the order stage. In the next chapter, we will talk about how you can make sure the script you order is the right one because many providers deliver the clone script. For now, I would like you to close this book and look up Netflix Clone scripts on Google and enjoy daydreaming about your own platform.

STEP SEVEN

SOLIDIFY YOUR

TECHNOLOGY

38. SEEK MORE SOLUTIONS
39. SEEK MORE OPTIONS
40. YOU CAN'T SECURE THE BAG WITHOUT SECURITY
41. MOBILE'S THE STYLE.
42. FAST, SLOW, LET IT GO.
43. DON'T TRAP YOURSELF IN NO GOOGLE LAND.

(!

Seek More Solutions

In the previous chapter, you learned about clone scripts and the fact that as long as you have hosting and get a domain name with 'unlimited bandwidth,' you can create your own Netflix. In this section, we will discuss what it takes to make your Netflix clone serve you better.

As you may have discovered from Googling the term, there aren't any visible prices. That is because coders create a close based on your preferences. Though the bulk of the code is pre-written, they include or exclude features based on what you are looking for.

What you don't want to do is rely on a single provider to set your anchor price. Depending on what the coder assumes of you, he or she might overcharge you or charge you fairly. The best way to get an idea of this is by clicking 'Get Quote Now' on various providers' websites. Don't lowball them too much because you want to be smart about the copyright issues that come with cloning wrongly.

Remember that everything about an app that faces the audience can potentially be copyrighted. The code itself, however, isn't. That is why businesses that create clones for hundreds of customers already know which elements to switch around to make the app and the website deliver the subscription video on demand website without infringing on any specific provider's copyright. But there also are coders who will literally copy-paste most of the code as it is and do nothing to change the user-facing side. As a result, they work less, get paid less, but open you up to liability.

Always seek more providers and ask for their prices but also ask, "what do you do to avoid copyright?" Remember that your biggest disadvantage is that you don't know how to code, and you want to neutralize that by making this script friendly for you. Just like customers can browse the app without knowing how to code, you should be able to upload content, create playlists, etc., without knowing how to code.

Ask the clone script provider you are working with what the upload options are. You want to have a back-end for yourself where you can upload content in as many ways as possible.

Direct Upload.

This is where you upload directly to the disk that hosts your website. As you start housing more content, you start using up more disk space. You want to have this ability regardless of whether this will be your preferred method.

Amazon S3 Bucket.

This is like iCloud but provided by Amazon instead of apple. This way, your content is hosted on a server on Amazon, and you use a link to embed the content into your platform's pages.

Link.

With this option, you can use any link to a video to embed it into your platform. Even if you don't use this method, you want to have the option. This way, you can use YouTube, Vimeo, or any other streaming service to host the content that people pay to watch on your platform. The only caveat here is that you want to make sure they can't get the links and easily distribute them. There are services like VimeoPro that make sure the only way to access content is through your platform.

Seek More Options

While it is well and good that you are on the hunt for more solutions when it comes to uploading more content, you also want to have more options when it comes to monetization.

Yes, I know that I back subscription video on demand, but what if you want to collaborate with a specific creator to provide a single, anticipated release. What would you do? The point is not that you have to monetize in multiple ways but that you want to have the option.

Here are some of the options you want to keep when getting yourself a cloned script.

Pay Per View.

This will come in handy if you get limited rights of popular content within your niche. It also is helpful when you are making revenue-share agreements because you are splitting the revenue from one creator with him or her. If you split profits from the entire subscription-base of your platform, you do not exactly have much of a perspective on what the creator deserves.

As popular as Money Heist is, do you think its producers deserve 50% of the cut of Netflix's revenue? Of course not. But if you pay for the privilege of seeing a fight between Connor McGregor and Jose Diaz, do you think the fighters deserve a cut of the pay per view money? Of course, they do, and they get it.

Subscription.

This is the model Netflix uses and must be your top priority. Once you spend money to get a customer, you don't want them to go away. For that, you have to do two things: create quality compelling content, and charge them automatically. And that's what subscription-based selling allows. Therefore, you have to make sure it is in the code.

Banner Ads.

I know I have discussed at length why Ads are a bad idea, but that does not take away from the fact that having the option is good. For example, a spoon is a bad hammer, but if that's the only thing you have, it's still better than nothing. And that is why despite it being a bad way to earn money, you still want to have the possibility to advertise.

Monetization strategies change with time, so I want to give a word of advice that I hope is timeless: Ask the coder what monetization methods are possible with the script and ask him or her to include options for each one.

And before we move to discuss actual payment in the next chapter, let's recap that you need to make sure that first and foremost, the script allows for subscription based monetization. You also should not settle for a script that doesn't allow pay per view method. Moreover, you should have the option to show ads, but it is advisable that you do not. And last but not least, monetization possibilities might change as the tech industry gets further advanced, so regardless of when you are reading this, ask the script-provider which monetization solutions are possible and then have all those options. The more options you have, the better.

You Can't Secure the Bag Without Security

When we shop online, we take payment security for granted. But it is critical that you understand that from the business end, you have to go the extra mile to make your payments secure. To explain this, let me take an example of your favorite product that you buy online.

Let's suppose the product you just can't live without is Sneakers. You can use any product as an example as you follow along with this thought experiment. If you can't live without getting yourself a pair of Nikes every few months, how willing would you be to buy the latest pair if the company demanded that you have to put your debit card in an envelope and give it to a random cab driver with instructions to go to their head office and come back after they've used your card to deduct the amount of the sale?

The point of using the absurd example was that while that is a physically possible monetization strategy, the lack of security would automatically make you want the product less.

Thankfully you don't have to ask the customer to do anything even remotely this risky. Because secure payment gateways exist, all you have to do is get the gateways integrated into your platform.

From Stripe to PayPal, many monetization gateways exist. You must ask the coder if the platform script has payment gateways embedded in them or the option to integrate them. If a coder is unable to deliver this, stop wasting your time with them. You want to be able to make money, and that isn't possible without a seamless, easy to use payment gateway. Here are some of the popular payment channels.

Paypal.

  Many businesses use PayPal to receive money online with PayPal 'shop now' buttons. While the service is versatile and you can integrate the button into any page with HTML coding, it charges a high fee.

Stripe.

  Stripe is a competitor to PayPal with a smaller fee but also a smaller range of embedding options. Furthermore, it is not available in certain countries in terms of receiving. So while customers might be able to pay from anywhere in the world, if your business is based in certain foreign countries, you might not be able to use stripe.

Square.

  While this processor is a little late to the game, it has a transparent fee that stands at 2.75% at the time of the writing of this book.

  All in all, you want to read up on multiple gateways and their terms and fee. Only then can you decide on one to choose for your platform. The thing with payment gateways is that unlike monetization strategies, you want to stick to one provider. The higher your overall revenue is going through one provider, the more incentives it will give you in terms of lower fees and better customer care. And with that said, as long as you avoid processors that charge over 3% and ones that allow monthly charges, you are good with just any secure gateway that can take all major credit and debit cards

('

Mobile's the Style.

This deserves a whole chapter because a miscommunication regarding this will impact the success of your platform. Remember that you want the code not just for a streaming website but also for streaming apps for mobile. While this may be a bit complicated to understand, all you need to know is that Netflix.com is a different software than the Netflix app.

Not only does the close provider give you the code that allows you to stream your content on a subscription video on demand website, but he or she must also deliver the code for an android app, for instance. You will not have to upload content to the app and the website separately, but you will need an app to submit to the Google Play Store.

The app will draw from the same source of content but will be more optimized for mobile. You will have to pay more for a service like this compared to just getting a dot com version of Netflix. But it is worth it as most of the streaming will happen on mobile. Here are some of the ways you will benefit from being on mobile.

Higher Engagement Time.

Netflix does not worry about HBO Max but is competing with Fortnite. Fortnite is a game while Netflix is a media streaming service. But it competes with the game solely because Fortnite has a high engagement time.

This proves that in the world of streaming, the longer you are in front of someone, the more advantage you have in terms of retaining them. Earlier, I mentioned your favorite milk brand. We were talking about the advantage of accessibility since the brand is most likely on the shelf of your local grocery store.

And in the example of McDonald's, we discussed the addictive nature of fast food.

But both those examples also present a compelling case for the power of habit. Those who form a habit of eating McDonald's become their most devout customers. The same applies to your favorite brand of anything you use daily.

By being on mobile, you are making sure that this is true for your customers. You allow them to access your service even when they are not hooked to their laptop or TV. And the more accessibility they have, the more they will use. And the more they use, the higher the possibility of them becoming permanent customers.

Go on a Ride.

Most people spend a lot of time commuting to and back from work. Though COVID-19 has changed this for certain offices, this is universally true in the absence of lockdowns. Even in places, this is not true; we do spend time doing things that require our sight but not our ears. This time is real estate. It is usually occupied by Spotify, but if you get someone interested in your podcast-tier content, you can be with them on mobile at all times. My average viewer spends more time with me every week than an average Netflix viewer. When it comes to your platform, you too won't try to beat Netflix in the number of users, but in the number of hours your subscribers spend with you.

) * *

Fast, Slow, Let it Go

VPN services help hide people's IP Addresses, so they are relatively anonymous online. It takes money to provide this service, so most VPN providers want to charge their customers for the privilege. However, their sales funnel involves providing the service for free with certain downgrades so that people pay and get the premium service.

Guess what the most common downgrade for free VPNs is? It is a slower browsing speed. No one wants their browsing speed to be slow, and the most annoying thing when watching or listening to content online is buffering pauses. Not only do pauses annoy people, but they also break their stream of attention and allow them the opportunity to opt for something else.

That is why you want a certain optimization in your content. You want to be able to make your content switch to a lower resolution if the customer's internet connection is slow. You need to correct for their internet issues because that's what being in business means.

Whenever their internet is slow, you want your streaming service to automatically convert their content to a lower resolution, so the continuity is not broken. But at the same time, you don't want to show them poor resolution if their internet picks back up.

For this, you will need the service to be able to convert to a higher resolution automatically if their internet speed allows it. Fortunately, you don't need to do much else other than communicating with the coder that you want this feature. If the coder is unable to provide it, do not get a clone script from him or her. Most close scripts come with this feature embedded.

)*)

Remember that coding platforms are oriented towards binging content, so you might need to curate the content uploading process towards binging. While on YouTube and other places you can get away with uploading content every week, you will need to upload pre-recorded 'seasons' of podcasts every few weeks. Furthermore, you will also need to stream weekly episodes of other content. So it turns out that you not only need to be streaming content at a good speed for fast and slow connections; you need to facilitate content consumption for fast and slow consumers.

Youtube is a great example of the resolution changing automatically based on your internet speed. As you may have seen, you don't have to upload a different quality video for each speed-tier. Youtube has a code that automatically converts videos based on internet speed. As for episodic content alongside entire season-releases, Netflix itself started doing that with certain talk shows and has moved to do that for certain series. The advantage of this is not just that you cater to both episodic viewers and binge-viewers. You also hook 'free trial' users to stay long enough even after their trial expires by giving them the fear of missing out on new episodes. More on this is discussed in later marketing and launch-related chapters. For now, keep in mind that both the code and the publishing schedule must accommodate higher and lower speeds in every way, be it in viewing habits or internet connections.

Don't Trap Yourself in No Google Land

Before we get to the point of this chapter, I want you to Google' Netflix House of cards.' What's the first result? House of cards Tv show's landing page on Netflix. While the content itself is behind a paywall, the landing page is not just open for everyone; it is SEO-friendly so that Google can see it.

How does Google find pages? It has robots that 'crawl' the web, and you make sure your Netflix clone allows not just for your site to be crawled but for each title to be crawled. In other words, I want people not just to find me when they search Antonio T Smith Jr. I want them to find my shows like 'Brick by Brick' when they search for them. It does not matter whether it is an ongoing show or a concluded one. I want the customers to look it up and find it.

That's what you have to do with your platform. If you get a script that puts the shows behind a paywall but also blocks Google's robots, you will end up with a platform that will only show up in results when googled by platform name. But when people search for your shows on Google, they will not get your platform.

Remember that when you advertise on Facebook, Google Adsense, or Youtube, people might remember a show title and not the platform name. You want them to be able to find you later on. Furthermore, you will collaborate with other content creators who have their own audience who might either google them or a specific show of theirs on your platform. Again, you want to be among the first results.

)*"

So how do you make sure you are not trapped in a 'No Google' land? You have to ask for a very specific term when you are discussing the clone script with your coder. You have to ask the provider to make sure the script has an SEO-friendly Architecture.

By asking for this, you will automatically communicate the concerns laid out in this chapter. If the provider says it is unlikely that you will not be able to provide this, you have to opt for another provider. Even if this means going back to other quotes or finding a new quote, this is critical because you are not creating a platform that will make only a few thousand dollars, you are setting yourself up to make millions, and for that, you need to take scalability into account.

When you are making hundreds of thousands and spending tens of thousands on advertising your specific titles and native content, you don't want people to look your content up only to find no results. Even worse is if they look up your show only to see pirates content

In conclusion, remember not to settle for anything other than a clone script with SEO-friendly architecture. And while you are at it, brush up on your SEO skills. Eventually, you will have a whole SEO team when your platform is big enough, but it doesn't hurt to learn more about it.

)*#

STEP EIGHT

LAUNCH

YOUR NETFLIX

) * $

Publish the Site and Upload the Initial Content

This is it; you are about to launch your platform! You have the content ready, and you got yourself a script provider who will deliver you a version of Netflix that is free of copyright issues. You have the layout and branding, and now you are about to get over the finish line. The coder will assist you in setting up the back-end for you to upload your content and will help you all the way to the point where the platform is up and running, only awaiting content uploads.

Change Passwords.

You will likely need to give the username and password of your domain provider and your internet hosting service to the coder. Once the coder is done setting up your service, you should login and change the password. If the clone-script provider finds the hosting service and the domain name registration service, make sure you ask them for the password and personally change the password and registered email for both.

What you don't want is to get the username and password for the upload portal but leave the coder in possession of the true back-end access. That would be like you have the same access as you do on Youtube.com now and the coder having the access that Google has to the source-end of YouTube. While the service might function, the coder might try to charge you monthly by being the middle-man and the host.

So here is the checklist to adhere to before concluding business with the coder:

) * %

- Get the username, and the password for the upload portal, then change it.

- Get the username and password for the hosting service, then change it.

- Get the username and password for the website name registration service, then change it.

With that settled, it is time to upload your content. You want to make sure there is enough content that someone can watch for a whole month. That is how you get viewers to stick around for a week. Not only do you want to upload that much content right off the bat, but you also want to make sure you consider that not everyone is going to watch everything, so you have to upload multiple shows.

After all, you don't want to lose someone as a customer if they don't like the show that you uploaded thirty episodes for. Instead, have three shows with ten episodes each. Remember, customers, love options. Even within the same niche, you want to give variety.

Who wants to see only one horror TV series? Which fan of adventure films has watched only one film within the genre? That's why you have to diversify your content and put enough of it online at the beginning.

In conclusion, remember to get complete access to your platform and then make sure that you have uploaded enough content for the launch marketing to be successful. Since you will be offering a free trial, you want to give people enough content that they have some left to watch after a week.

Collaborative Marketing

Remember earlier how we talked about getting content creators who have an audience get on board with you? Now is the time to leverage that for marketing. As soon as you launch, your content creators will simultaneously announce the existence of their content exclusive to your platform.

They will make sure everyone on their social media knows about it. One great way to maximize the buzz from this is to create an Instagram, a Facebook, and a Twitter page. Let's suppose Creator one has an Instagram account alongside the Youtube channel on which he uploads content. When he shouts out your platform on Instagram, he can simply tag your platform's Instagram account in the post and get some of his audience following your page.

As a result, people who don't immediately convert will still have an eye on you and may convert later on. Many people don't like to get off Instagram to sign up for things at the moment. But with enough exposure, they can, later on, log on from a laptop. This is where google-friendly architecture comes into play.

Many people will be finding out about your platform through content creators, and these content creators will give specific names to their shows. It is very important that they do not give their shows a generic name or a name that has already been taken.

The entire idea is to increase the number of ways in which people can discover you and join you. When it comes to content creators, aside from tagging your platform and linking to their content on your platform, they will also be consistently shouting out their series on your platform in their other

) *'

content. For instance, a YouTuber does a weekly show that gives people what they want every week but a certain passionate part of his base would rather pair a few dollars to be able to see his content every single day. If that creator gives you the ownership of his series and starts producing the content for you every week, he could end his video by saying thank you for watching. If you want to see my content daily, you can go to exampleplatform.com. And that is how you will not just market your product at the beginning but will have consistent traffic coming to your platform: remember how YouTube works. Some people are watching my videos that I made a whole five years ago, so those shout outs will always remain a source of traffic.

All in all, the collaborative marketing phase of your platform launch will be 'earned media' kind of coverage. When it comes to businesses, they have paid media, which is their advertising, and they have their earned media, which is organic. And with content creators, you will receive the marketing benefits of collaborating with them. This will make visible not only your platform but also your platform's social media. And that's how you start building the audience for growing one if you already have an audience

Affiliate Marketing

While collaborative marketing is the result of working with people who have a stake in your platform, affiliate marketing is basically incentivizing people to spread the word about your platform.

This is great because you are not relying on a few creators but potentially thousands of people who will pass on the word. What you have to be aware of is the fact that affiliates expect a huge cut of the audience they convert.

For this, you will need to actively track affiliates, and my favorite way of doing this is by using an affiliate tracking system. Since these systems come and go, I will not recommend one by name because that may make this book dated. So I recommend that you google 'Affiliate tracking system' and get yourself the right software to track which affiliate sent how many customers.

Another thing to be aware of is that affiliates have to be within the market you are looking to dominate. If you are in the horror stories podcasting space and you get affiliates elsewhere, no one makes any money, and this is not really productive.

But as mentioned earlier in the book, your customer is an ordinary person; you never know who may have a friend who is a horror fan. So make your affiliate signup easier and let as many people with proximity to your genre in.

One way to make sure you are getting the right people to market your brand is through age demographics. Many niches have a specific age group around which they cluster. All you have to do Is reach out to the general population within this

))*

demographic, and as they spread the word, they are bound to catch a few subscribers for you.

As for compensation structures, you don't even need to worry about it. Remember how I mentioned that McDonald's barely breaks even on the sale of a burger? Well, a free trial is the entry point of your sales funnel. This means you can let the affiliates keep 90 percent of the profit on the first month's sale. As long as this results in you making free money every month after that, you are golden. But that said, you don't have to give them 90%. Use your negotiation skills and get the best deal you can.

In conclusion, affiliate marketing is collaborative marketing where people who don't have anything other than a commission to gain help spread the word about your product or service. To make sure you get the right affiliates, focus on finding the right demographic when it comes to your target market. If your niche is populated by twenty-year-olds, simply opting to find 20-year-old affiliates will work. While not all their friends will be interested, the people who will be are likely to be in their social circle. And when it comes to compensation, be willing to give more on the first sale since you make 100% of the profit after it, and make sure to keep track of using affiliate tracking software.

)))

Email Marketing

While snazzy digital advertising and social media platforms may have you scoffing at email marketing, I still maintain that email marketing is the lifeblood of a business because the audience you have on any social media platform belongs to the platform.

Emails Have a Reach Advantage.

When Facebook started out with no ads, your posts would pretty much reach a hundred percent of your friends. But as the platform introduced ads, it became clearer that your newsfeed is real estate. To fit in ads, the algorithms started sorting users' news feed by engagement. As a result, you would see more posts from friends you engaged with more and little to no posts from friends you ignored once or twice.

So how does that affect you as a content creator? Well, it shows that if Facebook can take down your organic reach from nearly a hundred percent to 1%, it can push it further down to zero percent. Even if you spend millions of dollars to turn Facebook users into your 'Facebook Followers' the platform still gets to decide whether your posts reach them or not.

On the other hand, with email, as long as you don't spam people, your reach is a hundred percent. And depending on the open rate of emails, you get much better engagement than Facebook, Instagram, or Twitter. More importantly, you own the email list.

'

))!

What to Send in Your Emails?

You can send out weekly or monthly emails with roundups of the 'top shows of the week' and 'popular this month.' Furthermore, you can send high-conversion offers like "Halloween special: Subscribe within 24 hours to get 75% off for the next three months." And finally, you have new show launches that you can announce if you believe you can persuade the undecided potential customers to go over the fence. That said, you can be as creative as possible, and the aforementioned aren't the only emails you can send.

Whether to send emails weekly or monthly seems partially debatable, but since platforms like MailChimp allow you to see and sort email-receivers by subscriber-rate, you can simply segment your user-lists by two types of users. Those who open every email from you can be put on a weekly email list, while the ones who open your emails occasionally can get a monthly email.

How to Get the Emails?

Now that we have discussed the importance of having an email list and the content of your emails, the big question is how you can get the emails. The first way of getting emails is through the free-trial. Those who signup to your account and then cancel their subscription still leave their email with you. Include it in signup terms that you can market to them via email. And if they click 'agree' and signup, you are legally allowed to market to them. With that stated, if they are not engaging with your emails, remove them from the list because your email address is judged by inboxes like Gmail and Outlook based on how Gmail and live mail users engage with your material. If people give you permission to send them emails but still treat your emails as spam, you'll get blacklisted. Always, always, always deliver value.

))"

Digital Advertising

Digital advertising is a great way to market your platform. Earlier, we discussed the case study of Gaia, the Netflix of conspiracy theories. The entire platform was built by digital advertising. We also briefly went over Masterclass, the Netflix of celebrity-led education. That platform was built mostly on Facebook advertising. So you can really leverage digital advertising to build your audience even if you are starting from zero. But in your marketing, you have to keep in mind human psychology. In other words, platforms might come and go, but our primal psychology still remains the same. In this chapter, you will learn some of these decision-making glitches that you can leverage to persuade people to try your platform.

Pursuit of Pleasure.

Human beings are geared to pursue pleasure and what that means for you is that you have to target your ads to the people who already are interested in the type of content they like. If Gaia marketed to those who subscribe to academic journals, it would never have taken off. So know the niche you are in and make sure you target your ads accurately.

Fear of Missing Out.

Because we used to be hunters in times of cavemen, we didn't have refrigerators and supermarkets. As a result, any humans who were chill about missing out on a hunt starved to extinction. Pretty much every single ancestor of ours had a primal fear of missing out that ensured that their genes passed on thousands of years down to you.

What this means for you is that you can create limited-time offers and get many people to click. Since your product is digital, you can offer a limited-time free trial instead of an open-ended free-trial. This would make people want to try your platform right away instead of waiting and then forgetting about it.

Likability Bias.

Humans do irrational things for those they like but then rationalize them. In fact, we have gotten so good at false rationalizations that we don't even see our cognitive bias in this regard. The best place to see this is the political arena. When candidates of two opposing political parties do the same thing at different times, it is interesting to see the same people condemn one action and then downplay the other depending on who they like.

What this means for you is that you can rely on personality to market your platform. This could be your own personality if the platform is a podcast-tier content streaming service. It can be the personality of your content creators like Masterclass does when advertising through its celebrities' pages. It can even be with actors as Amazon prime does with behind-the-scenes talking head snippets.

Remember that McDonald's became one of the biggest brands in the world after Ray created the personality mascot, Ronald McDonald. So remember to use personality marketing but also leverage the fear of missing out and, more importantly, don't try to convert those who are uninterested and digitally preach to the choir that increasingly niched advertising allows you to reach.

STEP NINE

BECOME A

DISRUPTIVE FORCE

)) %

Go for an Audience No One Cares About

In this section, we are going to discuss domination through disruption. So you have to truly expand your mind beyond your income goals to take over Goliath. If you try to reach your income goals, you will find yourself motivated by 'getting.' On the other hand, if you are interested in taking over the market and destroying its sleeping giants, you will be focused on giving value. And that's a great place to be in as a business owner.

That said, if giving value was all it took to have the biggest corporation, Mother Teresa would have had the world's biggest charity. She didn't have it then; her legacy never converted into an organization the size of UNICEF. So it is time we get strategic.

The first step in your domination is to go for an audience no one cares about. But the very next step is to go for the concerns of your competitors' audience that they don't care about.

You need a few thousand subscribers to truly be in the game. So for that stage, you will need to focus on an extremely niched audience that is just too small for bigger giants to even think about. Some of the examples are horror story listeners, the audience in the self-help subcategories like mindset-development, and baking recipe viewers. Once you have a few thousand subscribers, you are going to expand your offerings and include a slightly broader range of content. For instance, instead of just baking content, you can have education on recipes about cooking Chinese cuisine and then

French cuisine. Along the way, you will be collecting multiple extreme niches that 'no one cares about.'

Once you do have a substantial audience, like a few hundred thousand viewers, you will need to look at your closest competitor. If you are in the podcasting space, you might be looking at barstool sports or even Spotify. In this, you cannot think small. When I say the closest competitor, I don't mean closest in size. I mean the closest in the type of content. So if you have a few Indie films on your platform, you're going to look at Netflix.

The next step is to google their app or their website's name. This will bring up reviews and ratings. And here, I want you to sort the reviews by the most critical. Read thousands of one-star reviews to find out what content-related or tech-related concerns the platform's audience has.

Make sure your platform alleviates those concerns, and you are ready to start grabbing the Goliath's market share, David. If people complain that a platform has too much old content with not enough new material, simply create an ad 'New material, every hour' and direct it at the users of the giant platform. The best part about competing with a giant is that his or her name is big enough that Facebook has an advertiser targeting option for it. Right now, you can advertise to people who like 'Netflix' on Facebook. So when it's time, the giant's audience will remain for the taking.

))'

Leverage FOMO

We briefly went over FOMO earlier in the book. The fear of missing out is primal, and in the chapter, we will look at different ways you can leverage this fear to get people to convert to subscribers and then stick to your service no matter what.

The FOMO Offer.

McDonald's can have the McRib year-round and make a lot of money, but if the McRib is available all the time, McDonald's doesn't have an ace up its sleeve to predictably increase its revenue anytime it needs. But how can it do that? By having some of its products be limited-time releases.

Because it is a physical goods business, it can even do a limited-quantity release, which we see with Kids' Meal merchandise. But who is to say you can't do the same? Not only can you release limited-time discounts on joining, but you can also release content that is available for a limited time.

For the longest period, this is exactly what live-broadcasting has done. After all, you can only watch a live event once. And Super Bowl has capitalized on this and, to this day, remains the largest advertising draw of all time. The NFL has even leveraged Twitter to create current conversations during the Super Bowl, so people comment on ads while they play. This has made the ad breaks during the Super Bowl as much of an unmissable event as the live sport.

The FOMO Habit.

Why do we log in to Facebook every day? Some of us don't feel good after scrolling through our Instagram feed, but that does not stop us from pulling our phones every few minutes. The culprit is FOMO. We have a fear of missing out on what's happening.

With exclusive content, you can leverage this fear to make your audience stick around. When TV was the only way to watch shows, many cable networks had a 'next on' epilogue to their shows' episodes. They wanted to make sure that you stuck around.

Netflix encouraged binging content, and so, most of its original shows end with Cliffhangers. Just to see what's happening in the next episode, you continue watching. To facilitate this, Netflix offers to help you skip credits of the episode you just watched and the intro of the next one. You want to adopt this, but more importantly, you want to make sure you have episodic releases that keep people waiting for the next week.

The FOMO Club.

The MET Gala is one of the best examples of genius unconventional marketing. When Anna Wintour took over the organization of the MET Gala, the Vogue Editor-In-Chief actively worked to turn it into a celebrity prestige conversation piece. As a result, celebrities would go to the ridiculous costume party with the most absurd attire just to be included. Outside of this context, you couldn't even pay them to wear these outfits.

You can leverage this need to be 'in the club' by creating exclusive groups where people can discuss the content and make memes about it. This will trigger a fear of missing out on the 'insider jokes' among people who come across the discussions and the memes.

) ! *

Tribe Marketing Can Build You a Cult.

In the previous chapter, we discussed the need to be included in the club. Here we will explore the tribal nature of human psychology and how you can use it to build a cult following for your platform.

From high school cliques to country clubs, we think in tribal terms, but what makes a club worthy of aspiring to be in? Think back about school days; what group did you want to be in? The cool group, I'm sure, but what lies underneath 'cool'? Social status. People aspire to be in a club that lifts their social status. So you have to curate your content and the conversations around that content to be 'cool.' Here are some of the ways you can do that:

- Have content that can be used to make memes.

- Have content that associates with pop culture.

- Have a Facebook group where you facilitate conversations.

- Have a subreddit on Reddit.com, where customers can talk about their experiences.

- Create media coverage by connecting with journalists and allowing them free access to your platform.

More than wanting to be a part of the tribe, it is the feeling of being in a tribe that is valuable. Here you have to start treating your customers like your family. And by making sure that people see value in being a part of the family, you start creating a bond.

When you upload enough content that people consume for hours on end, you are creating not just a family but are deepening that relationship by allowing people to become fanatics of your content while having a place to have conversations about it. This creates a powerful echo-chamber effect that surpasses anything giants can do.

Let's take the example of Drake, who was the biggest star in the world around the 2018 period. At that point, he had his rap audience and his singing audience. He had an audience that loved his romantic content and an audience that loved him flexing his money and status on a great beat. When your audience crosses hundreds of millions, you cannot make them feel like as much of a tribe as when you have a few thousand. And that's where a much smaller rapper XXXtentacion comes into the story. X had a few hundred thousand listeners on Soundcloud, and most made money from small live concerts in the mid-2000s.

But he had shared his life's story with them. They knew about how much he loved his mom, how he thought he was an ugly child, and so on. They were fanatics who would travel state to state just to experience multiple concerts. So you can guess what happened when Drake made a song that sounded similar to X's 'Look At Me.' X fans made sure everyone who heard Drake's song knew about it, and as a result, X got a surge of an audience that led him to superstardom. That, my readers, is the power of a cult following.

Putting the Leaders Out of Business

Business is not a game of comfort and security. Business is a game of domination. And in this chapter, I will make a case that you should always have a giant at the end of the road that you want to unseat. Many people get too complacent in a small 'sustainable' income coming from a business they have launched. But every sustainable, humble income can be snatched away. Only those who seek to dominate even have the opportunity to compete.

You can stick your head in the sand about competition or may even be okay with the competition. That does not change the fact that competition is a reality of business. It also doesn't change the fact that competition is for losers. What you want is to create a monopoly.

Yes, there are antitrust laws that prevent businesses from having a complete monopoly. What you want to do is create a monopoly within your category. The industry as a whole is called Subscription Video on Demand or paid streaming. If your business grows bigger than all the streaming services combined, the Antitrust guys are coming for you. But if your business is simply going for being the only documentary streaming platform or only podcast streaming platform, antitrust laws don't prevent that.

So don't let that be an excuse. You have to create a monopoly within your category and keep the 'competition' in its place. The other businesses within your space must know their place. And for that, once you overthrow the giant within the category, you will use the money you have to either completely buy out your rivals or buy a controlling stake in their businesses. That way, no matter how much they expand and grow, they will never overtake you.

At this point, you may be thinking, 'But Antonio, my niche doesn't have a competitor.' And that is good. Initially, you need to be in a niche where there are no competitors, but you will not just focus on securing that niche by keeping out competitors; you will also keep broadening your niche till you have a rival. For instance, if you podcast about jewelry, you can broaden by bringing on a creator who podcasts about art. Then you can expand to a niche of podcasting about creativity. And since creativity is open-ended, you can venture into film reviews, music reviews, etc. Ultimately you will become big enough to just be a podcasting platform. And when you do, you have to look at podcasting platforms around you. You have multiple rivals to unseat.

In the conclusion of this chapter, let's remember the essentials: you are going to get overthrown if you think competition is optional. You must not only create a business that brings you an income; you must keep your eyes on a giant at the end of the road. You must overthrow this rival and then acquire smaller competitors. This strategy has worked in the business for over a century and continues to work regardless of the medium.

Take Differentiation to an Extreme

In business, differentiation refers to making sure your product or service is not exactly like your rival's. That is because it takes energy to switch over from a business you engage with to a new business. So as a customer, you are unlikely to switch to a new business if it is not offering something different. As a business owner, this means that even though your business seems special to you because it is yours, you have to make it objectively different.

When you are creating your streaming service, you are doing it in a niche where you are most likely the first. When you are the first, you don't have to worry about differentiation. But from second to a millionth competitor, everyone has to be differentiated. Since the writing of this book, many may have been inspired to launch their platforms in various niches. So it is possible that a niche you pick may already have a competitor. Keep differentiation in mind.

One way to differentiate initially is based on exclusive content and your own personality. No one can be you. But as you earn revenue and become bigger, I want you to invest in research and development. While companies waste away millions of dollars in R&D, I will give you the secret to doing it on a budget: don't innovate just to innovate.

How many times have you come across an update on Facebook or YouTube, and you think, 'That's so inconvenient. Why would they change anything?' That's how most customers feel when companies change just to change.

What you must do is have your competitors' one-star reviews in front of you every day. You want to see what problems they are facing on the tech-side and the content side.

While you may not be able to fix the problem of the guy who said, 'Leaving a one-star review coz they killed off Jodie too early.' Jodie belongs to the rival, and you can't recreate the show to appease this customer. But many tech-related concerns will start to cluster around the same problem. That's where you can get a lightbulb moment and have the idea for a technology that is radically different.

Don't ever get discouraged by a lack of knowledge or expertise in coding because you can always find a coder to create the technology for you. I am a tech CEO, so I know that one can get a coder to help create an app, a feature, and or a website as long as one knows what he wants.

All in all, you have to remember to differentiate in content at the earlier stages and then create a radically new technology to completely disrupt the industry. That said, don't waste millions of dollars trying to create new things just to create new things; that will only backfire. While you must value creativity over best practices, you should make sure that all technology-related updates are 'fixing' the problems that your rivals' customers face.

Data and Disruption

While we discussed in the last chapter how you would look at rivals' reviews to figure out problems many people are facing, it is by looking at big data that you will get access to key insights that will help you truly disrupt the industry. Remember that Netflix was a DVD rental business that discovered the statistics of YouTube. In this chapter, we will go over multiple data points to keep in mind. When you get big enough, you will have at least one data scientist on your team, so you don't have to worry about looking up and keeping track of data points.

But for now, keep in mind the following sources of information that can lead to insights regarding data.

Competitor Financials.

When you are a public company, you are required to release your financials publicly so the shareholders can access them. But since your shares can be bought by anyone, you can't just limit the financial information just to the shareholders. Therefore, every public company's financial reports are publicly available for everyone to access.

You will look at your competitors as well as the broader industry leaders and see where they are spending their dollars. This will give you the general trend of where the industry is headed. Furthermore, you will see how much each competitor is investing in Research and Development so that you can focus on taking over the one that is lagging behind. If you work hard to create a technology that fixes a problem people are having with Netflix, but before you release it, Netflix launches its update and fixes the issue, what are you left with?

Your Own Analytics.

Here, I would recommend that you watch the Netflix documentary titled 'The Social Dilemma.' It is about social media algorithms that leverage machine learning to make users' homepages as appealing to their individual tastes as is possible. You must, at a certain stage in your business journey, leverage analytics, and machine learning to improve your users' experience. The end-goal is to get them addicted while making their friends want a taste.

You will not just look at your platform's analytics like watch time and user preferences but also the analytics on your social media. For each platform, see what is working and what that says about users' attention span, tastes, and preferences.

Qualitative Random Sampling.

While big data can help in seeing the overall massing, it is a human connection that helps you understand. So pick random audience members to hold one on one conversation with to see what they think of streaming in general and your platform. What they would fix and what they like in other platforms or what they like in your platform but don't see in others'.

Imagine getting a call from Jeff Bezos because he wants to get a first-hand account from you of your experience using the platform. You would tell all your friends. So not only will this be great for your understanding of the users' experience, but it will also build goodwill and positive PR.

Passion and Disruption

People talk about Uber in a way that is reductive of the problem that it solved. It isn't just an app that connects freelance drivers with people who need a ride. You must understand how passionately frustrated people were with cabs and the lack of customer-orientedness of the drivers in general. They truly had no option but to take this subpar service. On the other end, you have to consider the passion of those who were interested in earning side-income. They really wanted a few hundred extra bucks because that means some presents for their child that Christmas. And then look at Uber, and you can truly take in the disruption that happened.

There is no disruption without passion. Remember that there is positive passion and negative passion. Negative passion is the gift that keeps giving. The more people are annoyed by your competitors, the more opportunity you have to play the disruptive savior. But don't let that be the only passion you consider. Posting passion is what your audience is truly passionate about, and you can leverage that to make millions.

For instance, people are passionate about Disney's nostalgic classics. They remade them into live-action films, and some of the films grossed unexpected numbers. Netflix doubled down on the sleeper hit Money Heist, which was concluded by its second season. The company commissioned the production of season 3 and 4, and the story goes on.

So be careful about the products your customers are hurting for but also what they are annoyed by. And getting that information is half the battle. While big data analysis might show a lot, it is also the data most corporations are looking at.

I want you to befriend people within your audience, truly become accessible. That will get you raw knowledge that is exclusive to you as most CEOs like to only hang out with and speak to CEOs and executives. Why do you think that despite running a multi-million-dollar business, I leave my personal number public? Because if my customers or one of the readers of my book is hurting for a specific piece of information, a certain kind of guidance, I want to know, and I want to be able to deliver.

Remember that positive passion will usually guide you towards the products that people will love. And negative passion will let you know the 'solutions' that people will love.

When it comes to technology, you cannot rely on what people want to produce the next big thing. Steve Jobs created the iPhone when people didn't even know it was possible to have those features with that user-interface. You cannot rely on a positive passion for technological innovation. You have to look at a negative passion. Because while people limit the possibilities when thinking about what they want, they're frustrated when they are frustrated. And your tech can fix that. And if they want something, it is likely going to be a show, a collaboration, or a movie (i.e., non-tech product). Don't try to create solutions for every complaint. Measure complaints by volume and depth and fix what people hate most passionately.

) " *

What Disruptive Companies Have in Common

There is a battle against generalization, but without drawing patterns, we would never be able to make decisions. What happens when you give unsecured loans? You have to have a generalized idea to decide whether to give one or not. From generalization to scientifically valid pattern, the difference is in quantifying the common traits among a large enough data-set.

In this chapter, I will cover the traits most common among the truly disruptive businesses regardless of industry or time-period. The fact is that you may not remain in the streaming space as your business grows. So right at the beginning of your journey, I want to equip you with the knowledge to disrupt in any business you choose to go into.

They Understand Consumer Trends Before They Become Trends.

Disruptive companies are so intuitive about consumer trends that they give the illusion of creating consumer trends. That is because they know the key 'trend-setters' within their market and can see how these early adopters are behaving. They also spend millions of dollars on research and get the data that guides their omniscient decision-making. If you want to get access to data with millions of dollars behind it, simply buy a report from one of the larger research firms that have already done research in your market. It will cost a few hundred dollars.

They Focus on Smaller Markets First.

Airbnb started with one room and an air mattress, which is why it is called "Air" BnB. And when they started expanding, the founder went to local markets first. The mistake most businesses make is they try to capture the whole market and end up appearing too generic.

They Refine Their Business Model Before the Product.

One of the biggest challenges most startups face is that they aren't geared for scaling. With your streaming platform, if you are unable to scale, no company will be willing to buy you, and no smart investor would want a piece of your company. That is why I made sure your clone script has the ability to host content elsewhere so you can have infinite content. That is why having a secure payment gateway was important.

They Build Raving Fans That Take Them Into the Mainstream.

In this book, we already covered the story of a small rapper who had fans so fanatic that they made sure everyone knew about him. As a result, XXXtentacion became a mainstream superstar. But that's not just true for celebrities. Disruptive businesses have passionate early-adopters who act as propagators.

When the Fans Rave About Them, They Downplay It.

This one is a bonus trait that is largely true for personality brands that are disruptive. When fans rave about them, they either defer to the love of the fans or downplay it. This creates an even larger sense of presence because it seems like what people think is incredible about them is not a big deal for them

)"!

at all. Since you could be a podcasting-tier content streaming platform, this may be relevant and even necessary for you.

)""

STEP TEN

FOLLOW MY

$1BN PLAYBOOK

TO MARKETING YOUR OWN
VIDEO-ON-DEMAND
PLATFORM

)"#

)"$

Create a Traffic of Gratitude

When I was analyzing business trends and what businesses were doing to maximize their revenue, I stumbled across an insight that is relevant to this book but to disruptive businesses in general: while businesses in general focus on traffic of visibility, disruptive businesses focus on traffic of gratitude.

Businesses try to be as visible as possible to their potential customers in the hope that they can convert at least some of them into spending customers. However, the fact at the end of the day is that people buy emotionally, and disruptive businesses focus on giving people as many reasons to say 'thank you' as possible.

And this is not just true for small businesses. Look at Amazon. One-click purchase is a thing many want to say 'thank you' for. Because it makes life slightly easier. Then look at Amazon's grocery delivery service. That too is something one can say thank you for.

With that said, if Jeff Bezos flew down to give you a foot massage, you may be inclined to say thank you, but is it really a productive way to drum up business? Remember that at the end of the day, Amazon has a market category within which it exists. No matter how big it gets, it still has to make things easier within the space of 'shopping.' Its streaming service, on the other hand, is a different market category, and you can see that the ways they increase the traffic of gratitude are different.

You get Twitch premium with Amazon prime. You don't just get the option to watch content via monthly subscription; you get to rent only specific titles if you wish. Both of those are things people are thankful for.

So what are you going to do to increase the number of things for which people want to thank you? I would recommend keeping in mind that you are in the business of killing boredom. So how can you model Amazon and other disruptive businesses to accomplish this?

Increase the Number of Ways in Which People Can Do Things.

Within the context of streaming, you want to give them as many ways to kill boredom as possible. Each new show is potentially something that they can be thankful for. So really focus on finding new ways in which your category of the market share can kill boredom.

Decrease the Number of Steps It Takes to Do So.

One-click shopping is what Amazon did in the online shopping space, but in streaming, the provider bundled its streaming platforms, keeps creating new shows, and allows multiple methods of paying for content. So you have to make it convenient, flexible, and less time-consuming for your audience to engage in what they want to engage in.

All in all, remember not to just create different sources of traffic volume but diversify the ways in which you can gain their gratitude once they are your customers. However, you don't want to make them grateful for things that don't match your business and brand. And finally, make sure that you can make access to activity as convenient as possible.

Perception Matters

Many say 'fake it till you make it,' and that may be true in some contexts and not true in others. In streaming, authenticity sells. But you also have to balance that with making your company look like an attractive one. In this chapter, I want to make sure you understand how much perception matters and why you must look like a Fortune500 company even if you can't afford to do so.

Customers Don't Pay Strangers.

When you are walking on the street, if a man in a trench-coat walks up to you and says, "Hey, you want to buy some jewelry?" Do you immediately get into discussing rates? No. But if the same man is in a jewelry store, you buy from him, right? Wrong. You do not buy from him if he is in a trench-coat and looking shifty.

It turns out that we have a way of bringing 'stranger danger' into business if we do not meet the expectations of the customers. So if your platform doesn't look like a professional streaming service, people think 'stranger danger' and opt-out.

Investors Can Only See the Future.

When the pandemic happened, and the notorious 2020 lockdowns affected millions of businesses all over the world, every start-up pitch had one question. Want to guess? "Is this model pandemic-proof?" And that says a lot about investors. They can only see in terms of potential. When you show up to a pitch with a business that earns good money but looks like a sidewalk stall near a strip mall, you don't get treated like a company that can be a fortune500 company.

) " '

But if you show up with a business that looks like a fortune 500 company, they can see that it is not a fortune 500 company because they have your financials, but they know that it can be one. That's what IBM's founder said, that right off the bat; he started acting like the business he wanted IBM to eventually be.

It Is Good for Your Psychology.

I always say that your subconscious is like a quiet, observant child. It keeps looking at your own actions and how things are around you. And it uses this knowledge to create priorities. If you carry yourself like a fortune 500 company owner, your mind places more emphasis on business and allows you to make the right sacrifices and decisions.

Who wants to miss out on a fun weekend for a business that makes a hundred dollars a day? But if your business is a Fortune 500 company, you better believe you will stick around the office to work on it instead of wasting away the weekend.

In conclusion, let's recap the three crucial reasons why you want to look and act like a fortune 500 company long before you become one: your customers will be more willing to engage with you, investors will be more open to investing in you, and more importantly, you will be willing to invest in you. None of this involves faking; it involves carrying yourself and your business in a certain way.

Content's Audience Matters More Than the Content's 'Properness.'

Many of the people interested in this book are YouTubers and podcasters. And as a sizable portion of my audience is made up of business coaches, they may be interested in educational streaming platforms. This chapter is dedicated exclusively to such streamers because when it comes to podcasts, educational calls, and similar content, people care about the substance and not the other aspects.

If you are watching a TV show and all the actors look out of place or the set looks fake, it takes you out of the show's world. And that's what is important to realize; that in fiction TV, people care about the look because it is a part of what makes the show work. But in non-fiction TV, the right look will be nice, but if it isn't right, your core experience does not change.

So if you have live calls and your streaming platform provides an audience for them (remember you can embed links), then you have to stop worrying about making the zoom call look right, and you have to work towards making the content so compelling that more people are on the call.

A lot of the time, businesses just track the wrong number. In the world of free streaming, YouTubers worry about the number of views when they should be worried about watch time. In the world of paid-streaming, you care about the audience size, but instead, businesses are worried about making the background paint look nice.

A Word Regarding Consistency.

Remember that even though you don't want to prioritize the look over the substance, you don't want to be inconsistent with the look. People love consistency, and by having HD content one day and horrible quality the next, you create disappointment. So when you go high in quality, make sure you go when you can afford to upgrade the quality of every subsequent piece of content.

Other than that, you are good to go right now. If you are a Youtube streamer, a podcaster, or a coach, you don't have any reason not to launch your platform within two to three weeks because you are in the world where your content's 'quality' is defined by its substance and not its look.

Audio Is Senior to Video.

While in the world of fiction, media video and visual elements are so important many people forget that sound is engineered and everything from a punch to a step and the silence between dialogues is recorded separately. But in the world of streaming non-fiction content, the audio is much more important. So before you invest in an HD camera, get yourself a good quality microphone that makes you sound better.

All in all, it is important that you do not prioritize the look of your content over its substance and the best way to measure substance is by tracking the number of people who stick around. And if you are going to improve anything, make sure it is the audio first because people are consuming that at the core of your content.

Don't Just Differentiate in Product but Do So in Marketing as Well

This chapter's title is quite a mouthful, but every word in it is important. When we talk about differentiation, so many people get caught up in differentiating the product to an excellent degree, but then the marketing flops. As it is often said, "if a tree falls in a forest, and no one hears it fall, did it really fall?" The question is not a literal one but a pragmatic one.

So make sure when your tree falls, people hear about it. Let's explore some of the most powerful ways to differentiate your marketing. And since this chapter is about creativity, I will not spoon feed exact tactics but give you plenty to think about.

Reach Different.

Reaching people via Facebook, Instagram, YouTube is the new "traditional," so find creative ways of reaching someone. There's a great story about a jobseeker who dressed as a deliveryman and carried a box of pizzas to reach a CEO only to reveal that he was actually a jobseeker, and his CV was in the pizza box.

While that may work when you are trying to reach one person when you are trying to reach a niche, you will have to use a different tactic. The point of this section is to make you explore ways in which you can reach people within your niche without using digital advertising.

Differentiate Video Marketing.

  Using a regular video sales letter or creating traditional promos is so played out that it is invisible. You are spending your money to advertise something guaranteed to be ignored. Instead, take the example of Dollar Shave Club. The amazing startup had a founder who was a comedy writer, so he wrote amazing video ads and then featured in them. I highly recommend you watch those ads because they led his startup to multimillion-dollar acquisition.

Create Challenges.

  We spend so much time overcoming challenges that we run away from them. But on social media, a challenge refers to using game-theory to create a fun, viral, content-creation format. Let's look at some of the challenges that gained the most notoriety.

  The Ice Bucket Challenge – For ALS awareness, people would douse themselves in ice-cold water. The person featured would have the bucket dumped on himself and nominate others.

  Dalgona Coffee Challenge – The coffee that is easy to make yet beautiful to look at involves whipping sugar, water, and instant coffee powder to create a whipped cream of sorts. It is then spooned and placed over a glass of milk. A picture of this is posted on Instagram with the hashtag.

  TikTok makeover Challenges – There is a whole range of TikTok challenges where people do a before and after video that is spliced together to specific music. Usually, these challenges are named after the song.

All of these are formats in which people have to create content, and they are fun and not exactly hard labor. So think about how you can create fun challenges that people will propagate with either hashtags or nominations.

The Magic Number

We humans can't think about anything without filling the gaps in our knowledge with imagination or assumptions. Let's talk about my friend Christopher Clooney. The thing about Christopher Clooney is that he doesn't exist, but you already had a face in your mind. And you probably made it look like George Clooney because of the association in the last name.

This is what happens most of the time. There is no reason for a person who has the same name as another to have a similar face. But it is the gap in our knowledge that we fill just to engage in a narrative. So far, with this book, I am sure you have a vague target number of subscribers. It was either informed by your income needs and ideal pricing in mind or by associations like Mr. Clooney. You either associated your target number with Netflix's audience figures or with your current audience numbers.

This is the chapter where you get the magic number: Whatever you get from 3 million people on every platform. You should try your best to get there before you try to take over the market. If you try to get 50 million, you will not create a connection or a core base. If you try to get three hundred, you will not build a scalable business and get trapped in a dead-end.

So target your business to 3 million people. Make your business model scalable enough to handle 3 million customers. Here is why this is important.

Social Proof.

There is a theory called the mimetic theory, which suggests that all desire we have is created by mimicking each other. In short, people want things because others want them. And if everyone in the world immediately stopped liking something because others like it, we would all stop liking things altogether. While this may be partially true, we know that humans trust what other humans engage with. That's why we give our money to banks.

When it comes to streaming content, the best thing is that your social proof is visible. The number of followers on different platforms shows how many people love it. And how they talk about your content that is behind a paywall makes more people want to pay. According to my calculations, if you have three million followers on every platform, enough of them will convert to make your platform successful.

In conclusion, because of mimicking desire, the more people that follow you on an unpaid platform, the more the number of followers appears to them. And collectively, they look at this number and decide your platform is valuable and convert to paid subscribers. If there is a large amount of followers, they collectively decide that since you have a huge fanbase, there must be something great about the platform. So focus on getting three million people to follow you on every platform and provide them with content they love, in smaller bites, for free. All the best.

Streaming Is the Only Space Where Saturation Works

When it comes to making your streaming platform truly successful, you need to focus on content, content, content. You cannot reach a hundred million revenue without spending tens of millions on content. Yes, you may, at some point, need to spend that much money on content. For now, however, you need to spend time instead.

Create a schedule for producing content and stick to it. Produce content in bulk and convert everything into multiple pieces of content for maximum leverage.

Imagine subscribing to Netflix for a free trial and then having only one show to watch. Even with thirty shows to watch, a month-long trial would easily lead to you having watched all the content before the conclusion of the trial period.

Furthermore, you have to consider the possibility of not liking certain shows. What if you have one show on your platform that has seven hundred episodes? You would lose a customer instantly if they don't like that show. If you have three shows and they dislike two, they might just watch one and be done with their subscription.

You have to keep producing content in variety and volume, and you have to make sure you are tracking the analytics to do more of what your audience is loving and less of what they are skipping. There really is no way of finding out exactly which show will be a hit and which one a miss, but if you create enough, the hits will stick.

In the world of music, there is an example of the rap group The Migos. After their song, Bad and Boujee became a hit thanks to its micro success, which was only fueled by a shoutout from Donald Glover at an award show. The words "And thank you Migos, for creating bad and boujee" launched the rap trio to superstardom, and their Album Culture got a lot of play. However, their next album also had a lot of pressure on it. With so much riding on the anticipated second one, Migos leaned into the suspense and named the next album Culture 2.

And the album had 24 tracks. Yes, the group graduated from a 13 track album to 24 tracks. Their rationale was simple: if people want more, they give more. As a result, many of their songs became classics as different groups of people found appeal in different types of their tracks.

As your audience grows, you want to make sure different core groups remain satisfied. Saturate your platform with content, and then add some more. Since you can upload an unlimited amount of content, upload as much as you can, and of course, at some point, if you're a streamer or a podcaster, you'll not be able to provide as much content as people want, you will need to start buying content or hiring people to create it for you. You can use this opportunity to expand the market and get more people who are broadly related to your category under your wing.

Optimize for Voice Search

Voice search is quickly becoming the primary method of search. While the adoption of voice search is taking time to get on track to the mainstream, those who use it a few times become devout converts.

For this reason, I am projecting that voice search is going to be the main way in which consumers browse your catalog. Now, remember that while your streaming service might get a push by being voice-search friendly, you will get the maximum leverage by optimizing every technology that your company creates into a voice-enabled on.

Therefore, you don't want just voice-searching. You want your app to be able to respond to voice commands over the phone with Google Assistant. In the near future, it will be quite inexpensive to get a coder to optimize your app for voice. Imagine one of your subscribers walking down the road with his headphones on. He is enjoying an educational session, and suddenly someone he knows recognizes him and says hi. If your app is voice-responsive, all he has to do is say your app's name and the words' pause,' and it will stop playing.

Let's suppose your app's name is KnowledgeBump. At the time of writing this book, there's no such app, and if one is created since, let me say this is for illustration purposes with an imaginary app.

When the customer says 'KnowledgeBump pause," the person he just met will ask what knowledge bump is. While not everyone will ask people what KnowledgeBump is upon hearing "KnowledgeBum Pause," enough of them will, that it will propagate.

Expansion Opportunity.

Assistants like Amazon echo are becoming popular, and Amazon is getting into podcasting. This is where you have to pay attention to your competition. If you are a streamer, you should see how Amazon integrates podcasting and Amazon Echo, which is operated by Alexa's support.

I can easily predict that Amazon's podcasts will be available on Amazon echo. And people would just be able to enter a room and say, "Alexa play The Antonio T Smith Junior Podcast," and listen to it instantly. You have to make your app, SEO, and website work together to be as Alexa and Google Voice Assistant compatible as possible.

The Long and the Short Term.

In the long run, you want to have your own voice assistant that intuitively listens and responds to voice commands. In the medium to short term, you want the current voice assistants in the market to work with your platform. This is possible by discussing with a coder and optimizing your app.

For starters, let the coder know that you want the audio content of your streaming service to play on Alexa, like music. Furthermore, you want to let the coder know that not only do you want your app to pause when commanded, but you also want to create a voice assistant-like feature that responds to basic commands. This is a task that not many coders will be able to undertake as it requires machine learning. That is why you will seek out coders who are well versed in leveraging artificial intelligence.

) $*

Do No Wrong, Admit No Wrong

Many PR people try to convince business owners that they need to have crisis management that revolves around apologies and promises. But since PR people's first task is to ensure that they remain employed, there could be a conflict of interest that underlies such advice.

From my experience with successful businesses, the brands that are the best protected are ones that don't apologize. IF you make a mistake in your stream and accidentally went live in your living room for 12 hours, don't take it down and apologize; simply upload it with 'Acting unaware: a social experiment" and post the number of people who watched as the "results."

The first advantage of this is, of course, that you don't bring attention to mistakes and, as a result, avoid losing credibility. However, there is yet another benefit: you train your mind to think of positive spins. If you can do that with your business, you can do that with anything.

By constantly spinning mistakes to your advantage, you can become the person everyone knows is quick on his or her feet. There are multiple case studies of businesses that got something wrong but then spun it into an intentional victory.

For instance, the company that was producing viagra pills was looking to produce heart medication. The medicine was finally created after spending a lot of money on the research. During trials, the company discovered a side-effect: The patients were getting long-lasting erections. The company had two options. The first was to admit it messed up and apologize to the investors for wasting so much cash in developing the medicine.

The second was to spin the side effect into the purpose of the medicine and market it with a name like Viagra. Well, that's what they did. So the important lesson in this is to always try to get away with apologizing or admitting that something was a mistake.

Exercise:

Think back about the last time you personally messed up. Think of at least three ways in which you could convince someone it was part of a grander plan. What possible things could you say to communicate that it was something you wanted all along? Write these down. I would recommend you do this exercise every day till you are natural, and it seems like you cannot do anything wrong.

The Cross-Roads.

When it comes to doing no wrong and admitting no wrong, you have two options. The first is to simply ignore the mess-up and move on. This is one that I would recommend going with if the problem is not very visible. The second is the one where many people are paying attention to. In this, you have to find a way to convey that it was intentional and that you wanted things to go this way for a reason. A subset of conveying intentionality is to convey knowledge. If your business is buying a property or a brand and it fails, act like you knew this was a possibility and that you took measures to offset it. This is a type of admitting that you messed up without conveying that things can be out of your control. This is the last resort, and in almost all instances, my prescription is to do no wrong, admit no wrong.

Document, Don't Create

If you are a podcaster or a streamer, remember that all creativity blocks come from trying to create things from scratch. It turns out that creativity is not about creating; it's about cross-pollinating ideas. So forget about 'creation.' Focus on documenting.

Let's Talk About Different Types of Creative Content.

- News is documenting what is happening.

- Books are documenting phenomenon or stories

- Podcasting is documenting your day, certain events, or topics.

- Live Streaming is documenting an event or your opinions.

Even stories that are entirely works of fiction are a result of crossing different influences and previous stories we have heard. If your platform is going to produce fiction media, I recommend that you read the book 'Hero with a thousand faces' to learn more about how most stories are essentially the same. You can also do your research on Joseph Campbell, who looked at thousands of myths and found the formula for the character tropes that are common among them. Even he was documenting.

If you are creating non-fiction content, I want you to pause reading and rejoice because you don't even need to cross-pollinate ideas to create content. You just need to document. Here are some of the ways you can document.

Recap Past Events.

This is known as telling stories but really is recalling events. You can recap your day or bring up an event from your childhood; either way, you are documenting what happened. You can also find ways to phrase certain things unexpectedly; this creates humor.

Document Current Events.

You can Livestream experiences and create content in the process. Your reactions in real-time, as well as the novel occurrences, make for great content. Remember that many influencers literally document experiences for a living, so don't underestimate the power of this.

Document Your Opinions.

This is a powerful one, and an entire industry of solo podcasting is built on this. From the Young Turk on the left to Stefan Molyneux on the right, all political talking heads of the new media are engaging in this. But even I am documenting my opinions when I go live. IT's just not about politics and is about success because that's my market and my audience.

Document Conversations.

You have to pay attention to this because this made Joe Rogan a hundred million dollars. If you hang out with friends and laugh a lot, chances are, those conversations need to be documented. By simply filming what you are saying, you are engaging in content production. And the more content you can produce, the better it is.

In conclusion, I want to once again say that you can't have a creative block when you are not creating things from scratch.

And there is evidence that all creative endeavors are a result of cross-pollination of ideas and not the creation of things. So focus on documenting conversations, opinions, current events, and past ones to produce a bonafide portfolio of content that has people binging the moment they sign up for your service.

) $%

Work with Influencers

Since influencer marketing has become an industry in itself, I want to make sure you are equipped with the way to do influencer marketing. The worst thing you can do is imitate other businesses because they don't know what they are doing either and are imitating others. If all the businesses are adopting "influencers" by seeing each other, who is directing influencer marketing trends? Influencer agencies.

A multi-million-dollar industry called 'influencer management' has reared its head and has everything from faking user engagement to sending fake customers as a part of it.

Here are some of the guidelines that will best-equip you to use influencers instead of being used by influencers.

Work With Influencers Who Are Willing to Work as Affiliates.

Any influencer confident enough in his or her influence will work with a brand he or she believes in on a commission basis. After all, if you can convert and make more money, why would you rather make less money upfront? You're either not confident in the authenticity of your audience or are working with a business you don't believe in.

Smaller Influencers Are Better Influencers.

Work with smaller influencers who are more relevant to your niche than influencers who are too big. The reason is simple: Facebook and other platforms only allow a very small portion of one's followers to see their content. As a result, an influencer with 3 million followers may have only three thousand people who see his or her posts. Those followers may not even be within your niche. But if you find thirty micro-influencers with only a thousand followers each, you would get a much better reach. Furthermore, these influencers don't shout out brands as much, so their promotion has value. And finally, they are more willing to work on an affiliate basis.

Creators Are Influencers.

Earlier in the book, I talked about bringing other content creators on board to create content for your platform. You can leverage their influence by asking them to post about your platform on their social media. You may need to pay them extra for the shoutouts, but their promotion is the most relevant is their audience that sees most of their content is the only audience that will see that post thanks to the engagement-driven algorithm.

Customers Are Influencers.

I pay for advertising, and I get publicity for free as well, but no one advertises me better than the people who buy my content and my products. If you deliver value, your customers will become influencers. The goal of influencer marketing is not to select the biggest influencer; the goal is to get the most influence. And between getting an influencer who has a million followers and getting a million people who can influence one person each, I'd pick the latter. Authentic influence is the future of influencer marketing.

Influencer marketing is relatively new, and in the next chapter, we will discuss being the first but for now, just remember that influencer marketing isn't about influencers. It's about influence. So, find the influence you seek and then approach the person most likely to deliver it.

Be the First Mover With Every New Feature

You want to build a reputation as a leader and a trendsetter. You can't really do that if you ignore technology. Since you are going to be the first to adopt new features, you will need to know a few things that will make this process more efficient. This chapter is dedicated to making that possible.

Look at Emerging Technologies.

When the "hologram" of Tupac was brought out at Coachella, Kanye West already knew what he wanted to gift his wife for her birthday. And a few years later, the video of Robert Kardashian singing happy birthday to Kim Kardashian went viral. That's how geniuses think. "How can I leverage to make someone I love more grateful?"

Remember the part where I said disruptive companies diversify the ways for one to be grateful? Well, technology certainly will help with that. If you want your customers to be perpetually grateful, you will need to constantly innovate, and by subscribing to tech publications and reading tech news, you will be able to ask the question, "how can I use this?" more often. All it takes is to get one right answer, and your platform is the only thing people are talking about for days. Snapchat did that with the lens feature, and suddenly everyone was on Snapchat.

Look at Features Outside Your Industry.

Another source of inspiration is looking at what other companies are doing. For example, Tesla's auto-drive is nothing but bringing the Roomba (automatic vacuum cleaner) technology to cars. While there is no evidence that Elon Musk got inspired after watching programmed floor cleaners, using deep learning and artificial intelligence to enable auto-drive wasn't entirely unpredictable.

Don't Forget the Underlying Psychology.

When we discuss technology, we tend to forget that underneath it all, we still are humans who have the same tendencies. Humans are largely social, and we are status-seeking creatures. So when you are in the process of thinking up features or adopting ones that already exist, always ask yourself, "will this make my customers look good?"

Spotify introduced a year in recap feature, and of course, showcasing your music taste can make you look good if your taste is good.

Similarly, the memories feature on Facebook is as much for your friends as it is for you. After all, throwback pictures are meant to show off how much you have grown either in personality or, in cases of bodybuilders, in mass. Snapchat's lens feature enhances people's faces to be funny or more beautiful. Of course, people like to be funny and beautiful. If you make your customers look good, you will build virality into the feature.

In conclusion, it is crucial to remember that leaders in any industry are first movers with new features. I want you to take this further by being the true first-mover by being literally the first to bring new technology to your category. For this, you need to ask yourself two questions when reading up on tech news "how can I use this to make life more convenient for my customers?" and "how can I use this to make my customers look good."

Accept That the Internet Is a Miracle

Billions of people use the internet, yet only a few hundred thousand make good money off of it. By good money, I don't mean a full-time income; I mean multiple millions every year. Why is there such a gap when the people who make significant wealth online are using the knowledge that's already on the internet? That's because there is a difference in mindset, and with this chapter, I want to make sure you have the right one.

Internet and Scalability.

In the offline world, businesses need to rely on additional production, additional risk, and additional manpower to scale. Even then, at some point, the system would reach a breaking point and would need an overhaul to grow further. With the internet, PewDiePie's streaming brand makes $15 million in 2020. Streaming allows you to scale your audience without changing much on the manpower end. Because of the difference in scalability and revenue, anyone familiar with business and earning in the offline world can only see the internet as a miracle.

If you have not earned significant cash through a scalable brand online, you can't use your offline experience and mindset about money in the online world. You need to see the internet as a miracle to avoid getting in your own way when you earn more money.

Internet and Customization.

Earlier in the book, I have gone over how the internet changed the game by providing niched content and niched ads as opposed to the days of television, where soap operas and generic shows moved the culture. Everyone was treated as a mass, and most people acted as a mass.

But with the internet, more and more customized content, products, and ads are being pushed out every day. For someone who is used to businesses in the offline world, the assumption that he or she can target something as specific as 'entrepreneurs in their twenties who are shy and want to learn how to communicate' sounds absurd. In a world without the internet, you would not find enough customers and go under.

But the internet is a miracle that allows you to have seven thousand customers if your targeting is niched enough to be one in a billion. You have to think of the internet as a Genie's lamp that can get you in front of the customers you wish, no matter how specific the wish.

The Internet Does Not Wait.

And with all those upsides, I have to caution you regarding the negative implications of the internet. Since borders and distances are removed, and you have access to customers wherever they are and can pitch them very niche content, others can do the same as well. Going by the millions of copies of my previous books that have sold, chances are you're not the only one reading this. Furthermore, the internet is getting regulated increasingly, with Internet Service Providers even taking money from leading sites to increase the speed of browsing for them. All this means your success is time-sensitive.

Act now and start setting up your business, so you are ahead of others. Not only will this get you the first-choice loyalty from your specific niche, but it will also make sure you have a few million set aside by the time the internet changes to a space where only the rich can do business.

Respect the Super Relevant Platforms

Many people in life have friends of convenience. They have friends they don't choose based on values or interests but pick their social circle based on proximity. This is because of our decision-making bias called 'convenience bias.' Almost all social troubles occur because of this.

The reason this is relevant to business is that more entrepreneurs market based on convenience bias too. They market using the platforms they are familiar with and are mostly used to. In this chapter, I will make a case for why you should respect Instagram and TikTok. And if you read this by the time a new platform is super-relevant, then apply the same messaging to it.

Instagram Is the Super Bowl for the Millennials.

Millions of dollars are spent on commercials that the world would watch at Super Bowl. You don't even have to spend money to build a following on Instagram. This stark difference should make it obvious why you should respect Instagram.

When something is relevant enough to be there year-round, you can't ignore it. Many people are familiar with Facebook and would rather have only Facebook fans. I would encourage you to join TikTok as well. You can't just be on a platform you like when there are fans you can scoop up in places you are unfamiliar with.

Super Bowl ads are relevant because they are a conversation piece the next day. Hundreds of millions go into that because corporations respect the power of being relevant and being visible wherever the attention is. I'm here to tell you that you have to do the same on a scale you can afford. If something is super relevant, you better learn to be a part of it.

TikTok is different from Instagram, and right now is offering thousands of dollars in free advertising budget to those spending a few hundred dollars. By the time you read this, I am sure this will not be the case.

Let that be a lesson in how the internet rewards fast movers. Google started off by giving hundreds of dollars to each advertiser willing to work with it. Facebook did the same. All new platforms do. And when they have enough advertisers, they switch to charging and quit giving free vouchers. The same applies to the organic arena.

All platforms, from YouTube to TikTok, initially give immense reach to creators. When enough content creators hop on board, they don't have to incentivize anyone anymore, and then it's the creators who are battling for reach. No matter how late you are, it is still as early as you can be. Join today and take all relevant platforms super seriously today. Gary Vee advises people to watch hours of content on a platform before creating any because that allows you to be 'in' on the conversation instead of appearing like you are pushing your way into the club. I advise the same but urge you to get more niched. Consume the content within hashtags and searches relevant to your market, and then begin building a following by creating content.

Create Super Exclusivity

The more generic you make your service, the more watered down it has to be. As a result, you will need to not just get niched but get super exclusive with the benefits you provide for your service. Remember back when one could not get on Facebook without having a .edu email? That made Facebook unreachable for many and cool.

And then Facebook allowed people to invite friends, and you couldn't sign up without an invitation. That made the people pushing Facebook to their friends look good. Overall it was a great lesson in strategy. When you are small, you cannot afford to be 'big,' but you can afford to be 'hip.' So leverage that.

The Difference Between Exclusive Benefits and Super-Exclusive Benefits.

At this stage, you may be wondering what the term super-exclusive even means in relation to 'exclusive.' It's worth setting the record straight, so let's explore this. The strategy Facebook used gave people super-exclusive access to a platform with features better than MySpace. However, if someone clones a Facebook script and adopts the same strategy, it would not be giving its subscribers super-exclusive benefits. That's because any other platform already provides those exclusive benefits.

When Amazon allows its customers to buy with a single click, that's a super-exclusive benefit. But when all platforms have one-click pay, it becomes an exclusive benefit to each platform's audience.

To simplify this, anything you offer only to your subscribers is exclusive, but anything you offer to your customers – that no other business offers to their customers – is super-exclusive.

Super-Exclusivity in Effect.

Let's take into consideration what happens when you offer an exclusive benefit and what happens when the benefits are super-exclusive. With an exclusive benefit, you are likely to persuade a few undecided fence-sitters to crossover. On the other hand, super-exclusivity will make people break down doors to become a part of your service.

How to Master Super-Exclusivity.

You have to get creative with super-exclusive benefits, and any benefits I recommend here will be adopted and stop being super-exclusive. I will, therefore, guide you to the right questions you can ask when crafting benefits.

What Do They Want That They Don't Know They Want?

This is a million-dollar question. If you can provide customers with something they want that they didn't even know they wanted, you will have a super-exclusive benefit that can also be your main selling point. The best way to do this is to target a demographic that you are a part of.

What Can I Offer That Others Can't?

This is the reason why certain fashion and jewelry houses that are pretty small make more money than Supreme and Louis Vuitton. With being small comes the ability to craft an experience that larger competitors can't. The problem here is that it may be a benefit that is not scalable. So at some point, when you have the momentum, you may have to let go of super-exclusivity and rely on exclusivity, but till then, leverage what you have that others don't.

Tribe Marketing With Groups

Seth Godin popularized the concept of Tribe Marketing by emphasizing its importance in sustaining a business, retaining clients, and creating a sense of exclusivity. Among the brands that he admires as case studies of this is Harley Davidson. Tribe marketing is different when it comes to one's online business because, unlike a Harley, you can't show your streaming service off in the physical world.

This is where online tribe marketing comes into play. In this chapter, I'll cover one of the must-haves of creating a tribe with your customers: social media groups. However, let's briefly go over other ways in which online brands have leveraged tribe marketing.

Masterclass, Only Learn From the Best.

When it comes to Masterclass, by leveraging celebrity appeal and getting the top-most individuals of any field, the subscription video-on-demand service has created a sense of in-group among its users who feel like they're too good to learn from anyone but a leader within any field. Would you blame them if, instead of YouTubing recipes, you had Gordon Ramsay teach you how to make the main course?

Spotify, Look at My Music Tastes.

During road trips and at house parties, getting the aux privileges matter because you get to connect your phone to a speaker and display your music taste. Either the party vibes with it or someone scolds you for annoying everyone, regardless of your individual result, it's always nice to show off your collection when people like it. Spotify has leveraged this to an extreme by giving people recaps of their play history, which they can post on their social media stories.

Groups.

But none of the above are as potent as social media groups. With groups, you don't just create a tribe of people who are attached to a faceless label; you create a sense of true community. When you post content in groups, you are giving value and getting responses. This builds rapport much better than screenshots shared on social media. But what should you post? I have two main categories of content that are the best fit for social media groups, like LinkedIn and Facebook.

Addictive and Entertaining.

You have to post content that is entertaining to the degree that people type the name of your group in their search bar and open it before even seeing their default news feed. Addictive content spawns addictive commenters. Commenters are contributors who drive conversations within your groups. Soon, you will have people talking to each other and building bonds in your name. That is powerful.

Resourceful and Transferrable.

This category of content is helpful to your audience but also gives them something to look good in front of their friends. It's the same thing as being a part of an exclusive country club. By being a part of the group, they learn things that they can teach others and look good. They will feel grateful to you for this.

All in all, tribe marketing used to be all about the brand message and the logo, but since the physical world rarely sees who you connect to online, I recommend using Facebook and LinkedIn groups to give people helpful material they can share with friends and look good. And finally, give them addictive, entertaining content that they keep coming back for.

Never Sleep on Feedback

"The customer is always right," goes the saying that encapsulates the wisdom of centuries of business practices. In the age of streaming, this is truer than ever. Whenever a business has ignored its customers, it has done so with the comfort of knowing that the customers do not have another option. For instance, when your landlord decides not to fix the problems you complain about, it is very likely that you don't have alternatives within the rent range he charges you. But in the world of streaming, you charge around the same amount charged by Netflix and HBO. In other words, you can't afford to assume for a second that your customers won't switch if they aren't taken care of.

HBOMax and The Snyder Cut.

Let's take the case study of Zack Snyder, the director who brought a dark and gritty take on SuperMan to DC cinema. While his movies were moderate hits, Warner Brothers wasn't experiencing anywhere near the success Disney had with Marvel. In an attempt to capture Disney Magic, the studio brought Joss Whedon, the director of the first Avengers movie, from Marvel to DC.

This happened while Snyder was filming his Justice League film. Halfway through, fans learned that Whedon would finish the film. For months on end, fans rallied to get Warner Brothers to release Zack Snyder's cut of the film as they didn't like Whedon reshoots. The film, with Whedon's conclusion, did relatively well at the box office, but Snyder fans were not satisfied.

In 2020, it was announced that Zack Snyder would not just return to finish his cut of the movie but would be given four hours of screen time and a budget to reshoot scenes with the A-list actors. All of this just so fans can watch the cut on HBOMax. Let this be a sober reminder as to why fans' feedback is crucial to your platform's success. Even Warner is not too big to ignore fans in the world of streaming.

How to Gather Feedback.

Not everyone is blessed with a passionate and vocal fanbase as Snyder's. For your streaming service, you will need to personally canvas for feedback. Here are some ways to collect feedback.

- SurveyMonkey – SurveyMonkey allows you to create surveys for your fans to fill online. All you have to do is go to surveymonkey.com and register. Upon creating your survey, you will be given a link to share so people can take part in your survey.

- Feedback email – Do you know that you can leave feedback regarding Amazon Prime by emailing Jeff Bezos directly? Jeff@amazon.com is Bezos's direct email, and though he doesn't respond to every email, he randomly draws a few every day to keep his finger on the pulse.

- Facebook groups – Earlier in the book, it was recommended that you set up a group for your fans to interact in. This group will also be helpful in picking up valuable bits of feedback to help guide your platform's improvement.

- Reviews – Finally, we circle back to looking at reviews. Earlier, looking at negative reviews of competitors was established as a great way to learn how to improve your service. Let's not be blind to our own negative reviews and use them as a place to capture valuable lessons on elevating the user experience.

Attitude is Everything

Now that you have learned about the technical aspects as well as the content strategies, I would like to emphasize the importance of attitude in making your business successful. It is possible to get carried away in irrelevant details or to get overwhelmed by the smallest obstacles. Not everything will go according to your plan because if everything did, you would never stumble into opportunities you didn't plan for.

Keep an open mind and be flexible with your plans. After all, as long as you get the goal you set out to achieve, who cares what path you took? With your own journey, you must have an open mind, but with regards to your content-related decisions and marketing, you must be polarizing.

There are streaming services that try to be everything for everyone, and in my opinion, that isn't going to work. It does not matter how big a business or how exclusive the content; streaming is meant to remain a segmented voluntary-transaction market. You cannot bundle ten different services and expect me to pay for all because I am interested in one portion of the content.

When you know your market and stand by the boundaries you draw, you create a group of people who love you and a group that hates you. The people who love you get extreme in their passion, the more hate you get. As a result, you have committed fans who are willing to stay subscribed to your service because they relate to your values.

Gaia: No Apologies to Science.

Gaia is a streaming platform that has documentaries and podcast-tier content regarding conspiracy theories and new age thought. The platform knows that skeptics will not take it seriously. As a result, its marketing makes zero effort to answer any skeptic. According to the platform's attitude, if you're uninterested in the untold truth, then goodbye to you.

Masterclass: Not Your High School Class.

Masterclass markets its courses through the power of celebrity. While some programs have a technical element to them, most of them are akin to expensive interviews with celebrities. This criticism has been raised repeatedly. Has this made Masterclass reevaluated and release more technique-based classes? No, the company has since released a class on authentic expression and another on conversations. If you don't like soft-skills, then goodbye to you.

Netflix: Progressive Entertainment Won't Hit the Brakes.

Many American viewers have complained that Netflix originals intentionally replace the lead characters in their series to have the kind of casting that is unconventional for traditional Hollywood roles. Has Netflix addressed these criticisms regarding affirmative action in leading roles? No. Over 90% of leads in Netflix Originals have been non-white men, women, or LGBTQ+ characters.

In conclusion, I am no one to say that any of the above streaming services are making the right or wrong decision. What I can say is that they are all doing well to stay polarizing and keep their paying fanbase happy. Be polarizing, and don't ever address complaints from those who aren't your target audience.

) &&

Epilogue

Over the past seventy-three chapters, you have learned how you can get a subscription video-on-demand service. I made a strong case for why this is an industry you want to be in. And finally, we went over the step-by-step strategy to not just create your platform and fill its library but to launch it and have it be a marketing success.

But now we come to the moment of truth: will you do it? I expect one in every hundred people who read this to become a streaming millionaire. And the only difference between the one percent and the ninety-nine percent is going to be in action. Are you going to act? So I have decided to conclude this book by busting the top myths and excuses that will likely keep you from acting.

"I will do this later."

If you are planning to set this book aside and go about your day, chances are you will never return to the implementation stage. If you consider putting off the implementation phase, remember that someone else could enter the market you wish to penetrate. And whoever is first gets the majority of the revenue.

"I will think about it."

While thinking about any decision is a good idea, there is no commitment involved in asking coders the price of a Netflix clone script. You can start price shopping and think about the plan simultaneously.

"It is not for me."

If you have picked up this book, then it is for you. You may convince yourself that you aren't as interested, just to avoid the effort required but trust me, the effort is worth it.

"I am not good in front of the camera."

If this seems like a valid reason, you have probably skipped the part about securing rights to content created by others. I recommend going over that portion because not only is being in front of the camera unnecessary, but it is also not recommended if you can better employ your skills to get others to make content.

"I am just a content creator."

If you don't want to be a platform with hundreds of shows, you don't have to be. A clone script can still help you put your show behind a paywall for your super-fans. This is something you can do with Patreon as well, but then you don't get fans' emails as Patreon does. So between building an email list for yourself or letting Patreon build one off of your fandom, the choice is yours.

"This will take too much time."

I have clocked the process from A to Z, and it takes as little as eight weeks to get your streaming service off the ground. It took me twelve times more time just to research this book. But I went through with this project because I believe my readers can turn around their fortune with this knowledge. I recommend you commit at least eight weeks to this.

For all other excuses:

If your reason for not starting hasn't been addressed in this epilogue, text it to me on +1 409-500-1546, and I will let you

know why you should not let it stand in the way of your
streaming fortune.

)' *

About the Author

Antonio T. Smith Jr is an American Tech CEO and millionaire, who is on pace to become a billionaire by 2025, with headquarters on four different continents, and is creating 100,000 Millionaires while giving away $1.5 Billion by 2025. Antonio has created the world's #1 Millionaire Maker Platform, along with the world's first open source business university, powered by a disruptive tech company. Antonio is a best-selling author and a popular podcast host, with a show that reaches 70 countries and 60 different languages.

He is a self-made millionaire who started off as a 6-year-old homeless kid living in a dumpster and is now a celebrity business advisor who is running several multimillion-dollar businesses with the ultimate goal of creating 100,000 millionaires, making the worse sales person the top income earner, ending world hunger and ending thee student loan debt crisis.

)')

Connect With Me

Join our online community to stay inspired, network, and to find our ATS Community. Visit

VYBN: https://sharingourwealth.com/social/theatsjr

Text Me At +1-409-500-1546

Follow Me Online:

VYBN: https://sharingourwealth.com/social/theatsjr
Instagram: http://instagram.com/theatsjr
Facebook: http://facebook.com/theatsjr
Twitter: http://twitter.com/theatsjr
Podcast Apple | http://apple.co/2pAUvvZ
YouTube | http://bit.ly/SubPlzATS
SUPPORT ON PATREON: https://www.patreon.com/theatsjr

)'!